PEOPLE
IN THE **NEWS**

Drew Barrymore

by Anne E. Hill

Westfield Middle School
Media Center

Lucent Books, San Diego, CA

Titles in the People in the News series include:

Garth Brooks	Michael Jackson	Christopher Reeve
Sandra Bullock	Michael Jordan	The Rolling Stones
George W. Bush	Stephen King	Steven Spielberg
Jim Carrey	George Lucas	R. L. Stine
Tom Cruise	Dominique Moceanu	Jesse Ventura
Bill Gates	Rosie O'Donnell	Oprah Winfrey
John Grisham	Colin Powell	Tiger Woods
Jesse Jackson	Princess Diana	

To my "dream" mom—Words can't fully express how grateful I am to you for your encouragement, nurturing, and love.

Library of Congress Cataloging-in-Publication Data

Hill, Anne E.
  Drew Barrymore / by Anne E. Hill
    p. cm. — (People in the news)
  Includes bibliographical references and index.
  Summary: Profiles the life and career of actress Drew Barrymore, including her childhood and early fame, her experiences in drug rehabilitation and recovery, and her success as a major Hollywood star.
  ISBN 1-56006-831-0
  1. Barrymore, Drew—Juvenile literature. 2. Motion picture actors and actresses—United States—Biography—Juvenile literature. [1. Barrymore, Drew. 2. Actors and actresses. 3. Women–Biography.] I. Title. II. People in the news (San Diego, Calif.)
  PN2287.B29 H55   2001
791.43'028'092—dc21

                                                                  00–011398

Copyright © 2001 by Lucent Books, Inc.
P.O. Box 289011
San Diego, CA 92198-9011
Printed in the U.S.A.

Table of Contents

Foreword

FAME AND CELEBRITY are alluring. People are drawn to those who walk in fame's spotlight, whether they are known for great accomplishments or for notorious deeds. The lives of the famous pique public interest and attract attention, perhaps because their experiences seem in some ways so different from, yet in other ways so similar to, our own.

Newspapers, magazines, and television regularly capitalize on this fascination with celebrity by running profiles of famous people. For example, television programs such as *Entertainment Tonight* devote all of their programming to stories about entertainment and entertainers. Magazines such as *People* fill their pages with stories of the private lives of famous people. Even newspapers, newsmagazines, and television news frequently delve into the lives of well-known personalities. Despite the number of articles and programs, few provide more than a superficial glimpse at their subjects.

Lucent's People in the News series offers young readers a deeper look into the lives of today's newsmakers, the influences that have shaped them, and the impact they have had in their fields of endeavor and on other people's lives. The subjects of the series hail from many disciplines and walks of life. They include authors, musicians, athletes, political leaders, entertainers, entrepreneurs, and others who have made a mark on modern life and who, in many cases, will continue to do so for years to come.

These biographies are more than factual chronicles. Each book emphasizes the contributions, accomplishments, or deeds that have brought fame or notoriety to the individual and shows how that person has influenced modern life. Authors portray their subjects in a realistic, unsentimental light. For example, Bill Gates—the cofounder and chief executive officer of the software giant Microsoft—has been instrumental in making personal computers the most vital tool of the modern age. Few dispute his business savvy, his perseverance, or his technical expertise, yet critics say he is ruthless in his dealings with competitors and driven more by his desire to maintain Microsoft's dominance in the computer industry than by an interest in furthering technology.

In these books, young readers will encounter inspiring stories about real people who achieved success despite enormous obstacles. Oprah Winfrey—the most powerful, most watched, and wealthiest woman on television today—spent the first six years of her life in the care of her grandparents while her unwed mother sought work and a better life elsewhere. Her adolescence was colored by promiscuity, pregnancy at age fourteen, rape, and sexual abuse.

Each author documents and supports his or her work with an array of primary and secondary source quotations taken from diaries, letters, speeches, and interviews. All quotes are footnoted to show readers exactly how and where biographers derive their information and provide guidance for further research. The quotations enliven the text by giving readers eyewitness views of the life and accomplishments of each person covered in the People in the News series.

In addition, each book in the series includes photographs, annotated bibliographies, timelines, and comprehensive indexes. For both the casual reader and the student researcher, the People in the News series offers insight into the lives of today's newsmakers—people who shape the way we live, work, and play in the modern age.

Introduction

Living Up to a Legacy

Drew Barrymore is a member of one of the oldest and most respected show-business families. She comes from a long line of talent and, unfortunately, a long history of addiction. Only in her mid-twenties, she's fulfilled the Barrymore legacy of becoming both a successful actress and a drug and alcohol addict. What's even more surprising is that she accomplished both before she was even a teenager.

In 1982 seven-year-old Drew charmed audiences as Gertie in the blockbuster film *E.T. the Extra-Terrestrial*. That success led to late nights out at clubs and wild parties, where her celebrity allowed her to bend the rules and grow up too fast. She began drinking at age nine, smoking marijuana at ten, and snorting cocaine at twelve. At age thirteen Barrymore was in a drug and alcohol rehabilitation program trying to conquer her habits, going back and forth between clinging to life and contemplating suicide. At fourteen she became legally emancipated from her parents and began a life on her own.

Barrymore had always believed a fresh start was what she needed to create her happy ending. But even after starting over, she realized that life isn't always perfect. She's suffered relapses in her addiction, struggled with her weight, had career highs and lows, and been in and out of romantic relationships, including a less than two-month marriage to bar owner Jeremy Thomas. "It surprised me, I have to admit," Barrymore later wrote of her failed marriage. "I had fervently hoped for a nice, upbeat ending with no

Not long after her role as Gertie in the blockbuster film E.T. the Extra-Terrestrial, *Drew Barrymore began to abuse alcohol and drugs.*

loose ends, like in the movies, an ending that would leave me feeling quite the heroine. I really believed it was what I deserved."[1]

However, she's finally created a healthy, happy life. "The happiness comes from knowing that you're alive and have a fighting chance to enjoy it,"[2] she says. Barrymore's inner happiness has helped take her career to new heights. She's starred in more than thirty feature films, including the period romance *Ever After* and several comedies, one of which she also produced.

Yet that wasn't enough. She wanted to make the entertainment world—and her place in it—more worthwhile, a desire that led Barrymore to found her own production company, Flower Films, in 1994. "[Hollywood is] a shallow, inconsistent, competitive, cruel world," Barrymore revealed to a *Harper's Bazaar* magazine reporter in 1996.

> Whenever I get really sad that I'm involved in it, I feel
> that instead of sitting on the sidelines and complaining,
> I should go in there and make it better. I like making

movies, so I want to make good movies. I want to swim in a creative pool with wonderful people. And as a producer, I want to create a great working atmosphere for people, and I know how to do that. It's in my blood and in my bones.[3]

Although she has also let go of the drug and alcohol addiction that once plagued her, Barrymore has not completely toned down her wild-girl side. She still likes to have fun. Her antics have entertained and made headlines almost as much as her acting roles. Barrymore posed for *Playboy* magazine, flashed David Letterman on his late-night talk show, and claimed she was bisexual but hadn't met a woman who could hold her attention. Now, Barrymore seems ready to settle down with fiance Tom Green, and she's mentioned her desire to have children. There's not much in life that Barrymore hasn't experienced or doesn't plan to experience in the near future—and her entire future is before her. She has experienced much already, a fact that has aged her more quickly than time. As *Scream* producer Cary Woods told *People Weekly,* "Drew lives in dog years."[4]

Chapter 1

A Star Is Born

FROM THE MOMENT she was born on February 22, 1975, Drew Blythe Barrymore was famous. Her father, John Barrymore Jr., was part of a family of theater actors whose members have been well known for generations. However, although they were blessed with fame, fortune, and talent, the Barrymores also seemed cursed to live unhappy, reckless personal lives.

The youngest Barrymore quickly joined the ranks of being a famous entertainer. She had the same spark in front of the camera as her father and the same stage presence as her great-grandparents. These were her birthrights from the beginning.

Hollywood's Royal Family

Often dubbed Hollywood's royal family, the Barrymores' legacy can be traced back to the time of England's King George III, although the name *Barrymore* itself wasn't invented until the mid-1800s, when Drew's great-grandfather, Herbert Blythe, created the stage name Maurice Barrymore. Maurice and his wife, Georgiana Drew, called Georgie, were perhaps the most famous comedians of the nineteenth century. However, when they weren't onstage, the Barrymores' life was more tragic than funny. Maurice was a womanizer and an alcoholic. Despite the fact that the Barrymore marriage was plagued by his indiscretions, the couple stayed together and had three children: Lionel, born in 1878; Ethel, born in 1879; and John, born in 1882.

Growing up, the children rarely saw their parents. They were raised by their maternal grandmother, whom they called Mummum, and were sometimes visited by their uncle, John Drew, who was also an actor, dubbed "the First Gentleman of the American

Drew Barrymore's great-grandparents, Maurice and Georgiana, perhaps the most famous comedians of the nineteenth century.

Stage." The three young Barrymores were constantly influenced by their family legacy and ultimately followed their uncle and parents into the theater business, even though they each had dreams of following other creative career paths. Lionel and John wanted to be artists, and Ethel wanted to be a concert pianist.

When their mother died in 1892, the three Barrymore children were forced onstage by their grandmother. The family needed money since Maurice Barrymore spent all of his money on gifts for his many girlfriends and on alcohol. Maurice seemed to be straightening out when he married Mamie Floyd. But even though he stopped having so many affairs, he could not control his drinking. Furthermore, the aging actor didn't realize that Mamie had her eye on Maurice's youngest son, John. She ultimately seduced the fifteen-year-old boy. Soon after, John began drinking heavily. Little did he know, he was following in his father's footsteps of becoming a famous actor and an alcoholic.

Meanwhile, John's grandmother, his beloved Mummum, died. John's sadness only increased his dependency on alcohol. He watched his sister, Ethel, gain acclaim onstage as an internationally famous actress, and he realized, albeit reluctantly, that acting was probably the only way he could make a living; his name alone earned him parts onstage. Even though John tried to free himself of a trade he actually despised, he, too, followed the path the rest of his family had taken and became an actor.

John Barrymore Sr.

John's professional life was far more successful than his personal one (he married four times). He starred in several Broadway plays, and critics called him the greatest actor ever to play the title role in

William Shakespeare's *Hamlet*. He usually played conflicted, haunted young men, much like himself. Despite his success, John was soon lured out of the theater and onto a sound stage to try acting in a new form of entertainment: motion pictures—where he became one of the first screen stars.

John Barrymore Sr.'s success as an actor was accompanied by a turbulent personal life.

Although John's drinking influenced his day-to-day behavior, it didn't seem to affect his acting. His reputation as an actor grew, even as his personal life fell apart. John left his first wife to marry a pregnant lover in 1921. After endless fights, he soon divorced her as well. John met actress Dolores Costello on the set of *The Sea Beast;* she would become his third wife.

In 1932, when his and Dolores's son, John Jr., was born, John Sr. had already signed a ten-picture multi-million-dollar contract. He went on to star in such classics as *Grand Hotel, State's Attorney, Dinner at Eight,* and *Counsellor at Law.*

However, all of the actor's success couldn't stop him from losing himself to alcohol and reckless spending. When he died on May 29, 1942, sixty-year-old John Sr. was suffering from cirrhosis of the liver, kidney disease, intestinal problems, and pneumonia. And although he was often considered the most innately talented of his Barrymore siblings, he never lived up to the glimpses of genius he showed on-screen.

The Tragic Son

Although many in Hollywood mourned John Barrymore Sr.'s death, the loss was most profound on ten-year-old John Jr. John never really knew his father, but that didn't lessen his pain. While Dolores tried to shield John and his sister, Dede, from their father when he was alive because he was violent when he drank, she also kept them away from the entertainment world.

Despite his mother's efforts, part of John Jr. wanted to be just like his father, and when he was just sixteen, he decided he wanted to be an actor. Less than a year later, Barrymore signed a contract that paid him thirty thousand dollars per picture. The movie studio played up his debut, making plenty of references to the Barrymore legacy. With his good looks, charm, and inherent talent, Barrymore received good reviews for his first films. At his agent's suggestion, he changed his name to John Drew Barrymore, perhaps to differentiate himself from his father and his father's troubles.

But that turned out to be harder than simply changing his name. Years later, after having two children and seeing two mar-

Even though his mother tried to shield him from the entertainment industry, John Barrymore Jr. followed in his father's footsteps and became an actor.

riages fail, Barrymore had become wild, fueled by drugs and alcohol. He was arrested once for drunk driving and being involved in a hit-and-run accident. Instead of undergoing the psychiatric treatment that the court ordered as part of his sentence, John escaped to Rome, Italy, where he made movies and married an Italian star named Gabriella Palazzoli. They had a daughter, Blythe Barrymore, before their divorce in 1964.

When he returned to Hollywood, Barrymore did experience some success working briefly in the long-running series *Rawhide,* but his self-destructive behavior cut short any career longevity. His personal relationships also seemed doomed.

John and Jaid

Although he had met Ildyko Jaid Mako a couple of years earlier on a movie set, where she was a struggling actress and he was the star, Barrymore didn't show any real interest in the young brunette until later on. They were reacquainted at a club where Mako waitressed.

Mako was born in Germany in 1947 but was raised in Pennsylvania, the only child of Hungarian parents. Her father, an artist, and her mother, a concert violinist, divorced when Mako was young. A flamboyant girl, she was determined to go west and make it as an actress in Hollywood. After she graduated from high school, Mako packed her bags and headed to Los Angeles. In 1969, three years after she arrived, the twenty-one-year-old began dating Barrymore.

Prior to meeting Mako, Barrymore had lived the hippie life. He had given up all of his possessions and divided his time between a cave in the California desert and the streets of Hollywood, where he'd beg for money, often while drunk or high, his clothes in tatters and wearing no shoes.

Despite his disheveled appearance, however, he made a positive impression on Mako. "I was in shock, he was so mesmerizing," she recalled. "He had long white hair cascading down to his shoulders, ice-blue eyes and the grace of a cat. We stared and stared at each other. We had the most amazing chemistry."[5]

Little Girl Born

After several years of dating and living with friends, Barrymore and Mako settled into a small apartment and were married. There were problems almost from the start. John became physically and verbally abusive with Jaid after drinking or doing drugs. Yet as painful as his attacks were, Jaid never left her husband.

After she became pregnant with Drew in 1974, she believed John would calm down and be more tender toward her and their

An Unforgettable Meeting

As a child, Drew had very few encounters with her father. She often asked about him, but her mother always tried to avoid her questioning. One afternoon, when Drew was three, her father appeared at the door of her apartment. Drew recalled the unforgettable meeting in her autobiography, *Little Girl Lost:*

> He paused in the doorway, like he was making a dramatic entrance, and I think he said something, but he was so drunk, it was unintelligible. It sounded like a growl. We stood there, staring at him. I was so excited to see him. I was just coming to the age when I noticed that I didn't have a father like everyone else, and I wanted one. I didn't really know what my dad was like, but I learned real fast.
>
> In a blur of anger he roared into the room and threw my mom down on the ground. Then he turned on me. I didn't know what was happening. I was still excited to see him, still hearing the echo of my gleeful yell, "Daddy!" when he picked me up and threw me into the wall. Luckily, half of my body landed on the big sack of laundry and I wasn't hurt. But my dad didn't even look back after me. He turned and grabbed a bottle of tequila, he shattered a bunch of glasses, and then stormed out of the house.

unborn child. The pregnancy, though, only seemed to make John more violent. One night he beat the pregnant Jaid, kicking her in the stomach until a neighbor interfered and took the expectant mother to the hospital. By the time Drew was born just a few months later, John had already moved out of their apartment.

Although she was a young, struggling single mother, Jaid was determined to give her daughter love, comfort, and security. She temporarily put her acting career on hold to get a steady paycheck waitressing. She had to pay for the diapers, formula, and doctor visits her daughter needed. However, because Jaid didn't have a college degree or much work experience, she was often forced to hold down several low-paying jobs at once. Her absence had a profound effect on Drew, who later wrote in her autobiography, *Little Girl Lost,*

> I was too young to realize it, but my mother worked extremely hard so that I could have nice things. It wasn't because she wanted to. She worked during the day and she worked at night, which meant that even though she

didn't like it, I was left with a baby-sitter all the time. What effect that had on me at the time is hard to say. Later on, I resented it. I felt abandoned. But as a little baby I don't know that it mattered. Maybe it did. I suppose it did. I've been told that I was a very good baby, real easy and good-spirited. Maybe I just wanted whoever was taking care of me to like me.[6]

Drew Gets Her Start

Jaid was proud of her beautiful, happy baby. By eleven months old, Drew was good-natured, blonde, and dimpled—a perfect child. Others were constantly commenting on how adorable she was. For months, friends told Jaid that Drew should audition for commercials. But Jaid was reluctant to put her baby in show business so early on. She didn't want to exploit her, and Drew was too young to make any decisions for herself on the matter.

But, unbeknownst to Jaid, an insistent friend took snapshots of the baby and sent them to a children's agent. The agent was de-

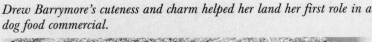

Drew Barrymore's cuteness and charm helped her land her first role in a dog food commercial.

termined to meet Drew and her mother. He finally convinced Jaid to meet him at a Hollywood sound stage and have Drew audition for a dog food commercial. When Drew's name was called, a puppy was brought into the room. Whether Drew got the part depended on her reaction to the puppy. Drew, it turned out, was delighted with the little dog, even after it bit her. After the unexpected nip, the toddler just paused and then threw her head back and laughed. The job was hers.

The money helped the struggling family, but Jaid still wanted her daughter to have a normal childhood, not one under the glare of Hollywood lights and paparazzi flash bulbs. In an effort to ensure this, she didn't agree to let Drew work again until a year and a half later, when her friend Stuart Margolin was making his directorial debut with the television movie *Suddenly Love*. Margolin needed a child for a small part in the film, and Drew got the job. The cast and crew were impressed with Drew's talent and abilities. They sensed that the youngest Barrymore understood what acting was all about—and they were right. Acting was in the little girl's blood.

A Career Decision

However, Drew was soon back to playing blocks in the living room of her apartment. Yet, despite her mother's reservations, Drew already liked being in front of the camera. She later recalled in her autobiography that, even early on, she loved acting:

> I loved being part of the group. Actually, I didn't just love it, I needed it. That's what drove me to club hopping later on. Being part of that really fun *in* group. As a little kid I was the girl who didn't think anyone loved her, which only inspired me to try to be accepted even more. When you make a movie, or work on any kind of production, I learned, you become part of a very close group. It's a lot like being in a family, a big extended family. And I loved that.[7]

Perhaps her desire to be accepted as a part of a big on-set family inspired four-year-old Drew to announce to her mother that she wanted to be an actress. Although Jaid was still wary of allowing Drew to be a child in Hollywood, she decided to consider the idea when she saw her daughter's determination. The two discussed the idea, and Jaid explained the pitfalls of show business—how hard it is to take continuous rejection, the worries that come from not knowing when the next check will arrive, and the odd hours. Drew was not discouraged. She said, "Mommy, I know it's too hard. That's why I want to do it."[8] Jaid was shocked by Drew's sincerity and seriousness. Ultimately, it was that conversation that convinced Jaid to let Drew give acting a try.

A struggling actress who knew how hard it was to get work, Jaid watched in amazement as her daughter landed the first four commercials for which she auditioned. Casting directors fell for Drew's charm, vivaciousness, and wholesome quality. Dressed in her bright, frilly pinafore dresses, Drew seemed the perfect little girl. She soon landed roles in two films, *Altered States* with William Hurt and *Bogie,* a biographical film about movie star Humphrey Bogart.

Even though she could charm the camera and crew when needed, Drew also remained grounded, participating in the same activities as other girls her age, such as dancing, drawing, roller skating, and playing dress up. Still, she realizes now that her childhood was different. She told *InStyle* magazine in November 2000, "My mom read Dostoyevsky and Henry Miller to me. We listened to Jim Morrison in the morning, not *Sesame Street.*"[9] It wasn't just the home life that made Drew different from her peers. Her talent also set her apart.

Learning the Family Tree

It was on the set of *Bogie* that five-year-old Drew first learned of her famous family. Jaid hadn't yet explained the Barrymore legacy to her daughter. However, the movie's director, Vincent Sherman, had worked with Drew's great-uncle Lionel and had known her grandfather John. Sherman told Drew stories about her relatives, and she wanted to hear whatever stories she could.

Drew learned that she had two older half sisters, Jessica and Blythe, who lived with their mothers. To this day, Drew has not met them. However, Drew did meet her half brother, John Barrymore III, whom she lovingly called Johnny. Johnny was twenty years older than Drew and lived nearby. Like his father, he was a drug addict, and he took advantage of Drew's adoration to get money from her. After he asked her for money several times, five-year-old Drew decided she would collect money on his behalf. She sold avocados and oranges from the tree in her backyard and gave Johnny the money when he asked for it. He told Drew he needed the cash for gas, but he used it for drugs instead. One day, after Jaid witnessed Johnny having a violent, drug-fueled outburst, she told him not to come back. She remembered what it was like living with Drew's father and knew all too well what could happen if she let Johnny be around Drew. She tried to explain to Drew that Johnny had a sickness, but Drew only felt like someone else had abandoned her.

Although she was just a child, Drew already knew disappointment from her father. One time, while entrusted to baby-sit his daughter, John stuck her hand into the flame of a candle. Often, he was drunk and didn't show up when promised. Drew quickly learned that her father could not be trusted and that her life would never be like the lives of her school friends or the children she read

Drew's mother, Jaid (right) kept her from visiting with her half brother, John (left), after Jaid witnessed one of his drug-fueled outbursts.

about in books. Those children, she thought, had two loving parents who never hurt anyone or let them down. Drew liked that world, the fantasies in her books, and she loved to retreat into it, constantly asking her mother to read from books like *Charlie and the Chocolate Factory, Eloise,* and *A Wrinkle in Time.*

The characters in those stories became her family and friends. And soon, Drew would hear one bedtime fantasy story that would change her life.

Chapter 2

The Life of a Celebrity

ONE NIGHT JAID brought home a script to read to her daughter. After reading it herself, she had quickly fallen for the story of an alien who befriends a young boy in a California suburb, and she knew Drew would like it, too. "I loved it. It sounds stupid, like a cliche, but I cried and I laughed and at the end, I got a real warm spot in my heart. I mean how could you not?"[10] Drew later recalled in her autobiography.

Drew immediately knew she wanted to play the youngest child, Gertie. She says, "I had a good feeling about *E.T.* On the way to the studio I told my mother that I really wanted to do it alone, I knew it would be fun. But I also knew that I could learn a lot from Steven [Spielberg, the movie's director]."[11]

What Barrymore didn't realize, however, was how quickly her life would change as a result of winning the part in *E.T. the Extra-Terrestrial*. She became an overnight celebrity, and like her family members before her, she soon learned there was no going back to a normal life.

Making *E.T.*

When she first auditioned for director Steven Spielberg, Drew displayed her vivid imagination by talking about a fictitious rock band, and the two chatted like old friends. Drew made Spielberg laugh with her obviously made-up stories. Although clearly impressed with the six-year-old, Spielberg asked that she come back for a second audition, or a callback, where she could interact with the two boys already cast in the parts of Gertie's older brothers.

At the callback, Drew met the young actors Henry Thomas and Robert MacNaughton. The three improvised some scenes. They were given an imaginary situation and asked to react. The three had instant chemistry. Spielberg was convinced that Drew was perfect for the role—if she could only do one more thing.

The role of Gertie involved a lot of screaming. When the character first meets the friendly alien, she's so frightened that all she can do is scream. Luckily, Drew was a natural screamer. The casting director and sound technicians told her she nearly broke the instruments during her test, where she screamed into a microphone. The part was hers.

Drew (left) won the part of Gertie in E.T. after director Steven Spielberg saw her chemistry with costars Henry Thomas and Robert MacNaughton (pictured).

The set of *E.T.* was special from the start. The group was making a feel-good family movie, and the mood seemed to spill over into the way the cast and crew interacted as well. On the set, Drew found what was missing in her life—a family. Everyone warmed to the precocious, imaginative little blonde-headed girl. MacNaughton and Thomas became like real brothers and Spielberg was the substitute father Drew so desperately wanted.

Spielberg often let Drew's imagination run wild, letting her improvise and add lines to certain scenes and asking her for her opinion on how they could make the movie better. For one scene, in which Elliot, the movie's main character, tells Gertie that only little kids can see the creature, Gertie's response is "Gimme a break!" However, that line wasn't in the script. Spielberg just let Drew respond naturally and the result was hilarious to viewers.

To a seven-year-old, filming *E.T.* was better than spending every day in an amusement park. Drew didn't seem to mind that her new world was a fantasy. To her, everything about the film seemed real, including the mechanical creature E.T. Drew talked to him during her lunch breaks and even tied a scarf around his neck so he wouldn't get cold. Drew later admitted in her autobiography that the three months spent filming were the happiest she had ever known. She wanted it to last forever.

Instant Recognition

Early reviews of the film had been good, but no one could have predicted its incredible success. Literally overnight Drew, MacNaughton, and Thomas became stars. The three were in the middle of a food fight at their hotel when they saw on television the long line of people waiting to get in on the opening night of the film. None of them could believe that their movie was causing so much excitement.

They also couldn't believe the whispers and stares that greeted them the following morning in the hotel's lobby. As Drew explains in her autobiography,

> The movie had been out one day and people were all around whispering, "Check them out. It's the kids from *E.T.* I'm telling you, that's the little girl from the movie." Every

place we went, we were followed. People asked for auto-graphs. They stared. They knew my name. They wanted to talk to me. They asked me to tell them what E.T. was *really* like. I thought it was insane. I didn't know how to deal with it, and that frightened me.[12]

It was a lot for Drew to take in at the time, but she was aware that her life had changed. She felt a mix of emotions: She felt ex-hilarated, scared, and lonely because everything had happened so fast. Magazines ran stories on the seven-year-old—the youngest Barrymore and the latest to be in the public spotlight. Suddenly Drew found it impossible not to hear about her famous family. Comparisons were drawn all the time between her and her ances-tors. People wanted to know everything from her favorite color to

Drew found herself showered with attention from both the media and the general public after the release of E.T.

Drew Finds a Substitute Father

Drew Barrymore feels that Steven Spielberg is, in many ways, the father she never had.

Perhaps the most important thing Drew learned on the set of *E.T.* was how to relate to a father figure. Even since their meeting in 1980, Drew and director Steven Spielberg have remained close. He was even named her godfather. Drew describes their relationship in *Little Girl Lost*.

Right off, I fell in love with Steven. In many ways he was—and always will be—the dad I never had. I wanted so badly to be accepted by him, and when I was, it meant a lot to me. I was thrilled when he invited me to his Malibu house. We'd run along the beach, collect seashells, and build sand castles. It was so much fun to hang out with him.

He'd often take me aside and say something like "You're talking to me now. So you really like this? Or do you have a different idea? Do you think it could be done a different way?" Eventually, I'd add something and Steven would smile and say, "Good let's combine ideas." It made me feel so good. For once, I didn't feel like some stupid little kid trying to make people love me. I felt important and useful. . . .

Steven is also responsible for the best advice I've ever been given in acting—actually, on anything. One time he told me, "Drew, you can't act your character, you've got to be your character." . . . It's amazing how one brief sentence like that—don't act your character, be your character, don't act like you imagine yourself, be yourself—can be so profound and make such a difference in your life.

her favorite food. And they all wanted to know what she thought of her famous family. Drew reveals in her autobiography, "What could I say? I'd never met them. I just smiled and said they were great and I hoped one day I would be considered as accomplished as them."[13]

The summer that *E.T.* was released, the post office issued a commemorative stamp featuring the Barrymore family. The stamp was unveiled during a ceremony at the Shubert Theater in New York City. Afterward, there was a party to celebrate the event. Jaid accompanied Drew, who wore a long white dress and a bow in her hair. Amidst all of the famous celebrities in attendance, Drew was singled out and called the new generation of Barrymores. It was a significant moment in her life. She was suddenly being examined as an actress from a famous family and not just regarded as a regular kid, a fact that would haunt her later on. That night, however, Drew relished the attention lavished on her. She says, "I felt strangely connected to all of that heritage—strangely because it was only through the complete accident of birth and nothing I did. Yet I felt it, and, I suppose, subconsciously began to assume the role of the latest Barrymore actor, which was a lot to live up to."[14]

Late Nights for a Little Girl

But parties and events soon became more frequent. As a celebrity, there were endless invitations, and Drew was usually out late with her mother, who enjoyed mingling with celebrities and feeling important. Although the parties did hold a certain excitement for her at first, usually Drew would have rather been at home, listening to a bedtime story.

On one of those late nights, Drew hosted the comedy show *Saturday Night Live.* As the show's youngest-ever guest host, the seven-year-old was nervous. But the cast members made her relax, and having Steven Spielberg sitting in the front row helped, too.

Then, it was off for a month-long international promotional tour to promote *E.T.* When she returned to the United States, Drew had just two days to catch her breath before finishing her first-grade year at the Fountain Day School. The classroom to which she returned, though, would never be the same. All of her

Even though she was only seven years old, invitations to various parties and events became frequent after Drew became a star.

classmates and most of the teachers and their families had seen *E.T.* over the summer. Many of the teachers were impressed and asked for Drew's autograph. The students, however, were jealous and ridiculed Drew behind her back. Suddenly fame had singled her out as someone different, when all Drew really wanted was to fit in. She didn't have a normal family life, and after *E.T.* she was even more different from her classmates. Her career was just something else that made her unusual.

Problems at Work and at Home

To make things even worse, Drew's parents were in the midst of a messy divorce. Although they hadn't lived together since Drew was born, the two were still technically married. Jaid wanted sole custody of her daughter, but for reasons Drew and her mother never understood, John wouldn't sign the papers. One night, after John had a confrontation with her mother, Drew lost her temper with her drunken father. She had had enough of his physical and verbal abuse. Perhaps buoyed by confidence after being accepted by her castmates in *E.T.*, she told him she never wanted to see him again. Indeed, it was almost seven years before their next meeting.

While her parents fought it out, Drew came to an important decision: She wanted to continue acting. With Drew's $75,000 paycheck for *E.T.*, Jaid was able to quit working so much and began managing her daughter's career, taking Drew to auditions and helping her with her lines. The next role Drew landed, for the movie *Irreconcilable Differences,* mirrored her troubled home life. She played Casey, a girl caught between her bickering parents. Instead of just painfully watching, however, the nine-year-old character decides to try to legally divorce her parents, played by actors Shelley Long and Ryan O'Neal.

Maybe the sad storyline of two people unable to live together anymore affected the moods of those involved, because instead of the happiness that presided over the set of *E.T.*, everyone fought over camera angles and scenes. Numerous takes were required for even the most simple scene. Drew recalled one such scene that involved her character: "There was one particular shot—not even a scene, just a tiny shot—that involved me, and it took us somewhere in the neighborhood of forty takes before everyone involved was satisfied. By that point I was so emotionally drained that I broke down and cried."[15]

When filming ended, Jaid and Drew moved from their small West Hollywood home to a nicer house in the more prestigious San Fernando Valley. Drew also started at a new school, Westland. As the new kid at school—coupled with the fact that she was famous—she was subject to even more teasing and ridicule than she'd encountered at Fountain Day. She struggled to fit in and eventually made a few friends with her shy, sincere sense of humor.

But Drew wanted to get back into acting despite the troubles on her last film. Her mother found a new script for her, and Drew was ready to give it a try. The new film, *Firestarter,* was based on a horror novel by writer Stephen King and costarred such well-known Hollywood actors as Martin Sheen and George C. Scott.

This time, Drew would be the star, playing a little girl with the ability to set things on fire just by concentrating on them. In the summer of 1983, mother and daughter traveled to North Carolina for the three and a half months of filming.

During the filming of Firestarter, *Drew developed close relationships with several people on the set.*

Firestarter

Drew, who usually wasn't very comfortable with changes, was thrilled with her new surroundings, which included a nice home in a wooded neighborhood. The work, however, was intense. Drew often slept during the day and filmed all night, as many of the scenes required a nighttime setting. Many of the scenes also involved dangerous stunts, typically involving fire, and special effects. Drew eventually got used to seeing stunt people burst into flames before her eyes. At first, though, she didn't realize that they were wearing protective suits. As Drew later explained,

> At one point, my double [someone who stands in for an actor when he or she can't be present] and I were instructed to stand and watch the special effects people set this stuntman on fire. . . . This was supposed to ease my fear. The stuntman, they told us, would burn nothing more than a match flame. But this guy just exploded—I mean burst—into huge, leaping flames, and we freaked. My double and I screamed and held on to each other, trying not to cry. It seemed like a disaster, like the guy was being fried right in front of us, and everyone was clapping. We didn't realize the stuntman was protected. But then the fire was extinguished and he popped out smiling, "Is it hot out, or is it just me?" he asked.[16]

Drew soon got used to the camaraderie she had missed on her last movie set. Although her nights were long and tiring, everything else seemed perfect. Drew had a good time and made many friends. She liked her costar, legendary actor George C. Scott, whom she claimed looked big and frightening, but was really gentle and friendly. She also grew very close to Stephen King. The two would talk for hours about movies and indulge in their love of hamburgers at lunch. King had children around Barrymore's age, and she was a frequent guest in their home.

By far, though, the closest friendship Barrymore made during filming was with her stand-in, Jenny Ward. A stand-in is someone of similar age, height, and appearance to a film's star who's hired to literally stand in for them during rehearsals where there will be a lot of waiting. Jenny's family lived in the area, and Drew and Jaid's rental home was in their neighborhood. Drew admits that Jenny was the kind of girl she wanted to be. She had a nice home with two parents and a younger brother. Jenny seemed to be popular with her classmates, too. Drew found herself spending more and more time at the Wards' home. She ate dinner there, spent the night, and even went to church and ran errands with them.

The First Drink

The amount of time she spent with Jenny and the Wards made the completion of filming very hard to bear. At the cast party to celebrate filming's completion, Barrymore was especially sad. At that party, Drew tried alcohol for the first time, perhaps, she speculates, in an effort to forget her problems. She approached two men who were on the film's crew and claimed she could down two glasses of champagne. Although they were skeptical at first, the two men agreed to let her try. "I took the crystal glass and studied it for a moment," Drew recalled in her autobiography. "There wasn't that much in it, I thought. It was bubbling. It looked pretty, refreshing." [17] The next thing Drew knew, she was lying on a couch and being asked if she was all right. She hadn't eaten very much that night and had passed out from the effects of the alcohol. When she admitted to drinking the champagne, her mother insisted that she not do it again.

Drew meant to obey her mother; however, once she was back in Los Angeles, there were invitations to more parties. Jaid and Drew were out late a few nights a week. Although she later had regrets about taking little Drew out, Jaid enjoyed the parties; it seemed a good way to mingle and network. Many of Hollywood's directors, producers, and casting agents were at the clubs and parties. A meeting or introduction was a good way to get cast in a film.

Because Drew was always the youngest person in the room, adults found her adorable and often spoke candidly around her, thinking mature subjects were far over her head. Drew learned about sex and drugs at these parties. But she never heard the whole story, so she often felt more naive than informed. The party scene affected Drew's childhood, and she grew up way too fast.

It was hard for Drew to ignore that everyone who was drinking seemed to be having a great time. She was anxious to start drinking so she, too, could have fun. It was frustrating, though, because she knew that she was too young and didn't exactly fit in at the parties she attended.

But she also didn't fit in at her new school, where she struggled to keep a C-minus average. She wasn't very popular with the students—or the teachers. Instead of giving her more attention, teachers gave up on her, claiming she'd obviously chosen a career over an education. Drew was smart, but she simply didn't feel as stimulated in the classroom as she did on a movie set. She wasn't motivated by the classroom setting. However, on a movie set, she says, "I desperately wanted to excel, even if it meant expending every last ounce of energy." [18]

Back to Work

Drew's wish to get out of school came true that summer when she returned to North Carolina to film another Stephen King film, *Cat's Eye*. She was back to the work she loved and the friend she'd missed. Jenny was just the same as Drew remembered, but Drew herself had changed. She recalls in her book, "I spoke differently, using a lot of slang I'd picked up in Los Angeles, and I talked about things that just weren't part of her world, like the Carson show, various clubs I'd been to, and entertainers I'd met. It wasn't intentional. I wasn't trying to make myself seem better than I was. That was my life." [19]

Soon, though, those differences no longer mattered, and Drew was a normal nine-year-old again, playing dolls and dress up. Hollywood seemed a million miles away. She didn't miss her life there, and she was grateful for acting and the chance to be a part of a group. The cast and crew of *Cat's Eye* were like another makeshift family. King visited the set, and the Wards were like her own relatives—the ones she'd always wanted. "They were a fantasy brought to life," Drew says. "A dream. My dream. Only the next day I'd wake up and it would all be over." [20]

When filming ended, Drew was again crushed. By the time she got back to California, she was desperately unhappy. She spent the

After struggling in school, Drew was happy to return to North Carolina to film Cat's Eye.

next few months struggling with her schoolwork, being teased because of her weight (she still had some baby fat), and attending an
endless whirlwind of parties where she felt accepted and loved.

At these parties, people went out of their way to talk to her
and she was often the center of attention. The adults seemed so
happy, and Drew and her best friend, Gigi, whose mother was a
friend of Jaid's, wanted to be like them. Both girls came from single-parent homes and lacked supervision. Together, they often got

into trouble and fantasized about what life would be like when they grew up. "Twenty one became my magic number," Drew remembers. "Adults, I figured didn't have to answer to anyone, they didn't have to follow rules. My role models were those people I saw at clubs, dressed up, laughing, carrying a drink, staying out to two or three in the morning. They seemed to have all the fun, and I didn't have any. Or at least, not enough."[21]

A Preteen Alcoholic

Drew and Gigi began smoking in the bathroom before they went out at night. Then, Drew reasoned that she might as well drink also since adults usually did both at the same time. The Hollywood clubs she went to with her mom, Gigi, and Gigi's mom were the perfect place to experiment. At a birthday party for actor Rob Lowe, for example, Drew and Gigi stole a beer from the bar and chugged it in a bathroom stall. Drew then conned another party-goer by asking if she could have a sip of his beer. She finished his bottle.

Drew clearly loved the party lifestyle. At the clubs, she became another person—one who was older, sophisticated, popular— even if it was only for a night. She and Gigi would dress up like adults, wearing lots of make up, low-cut dresses, and high heels. Instead of making her change and take off the makeup, Jaid thought Drew and her friend looked adorable, and she told them so. Both Barrymores became a regular fixture at many of Hollywood's and New York City's trendiest clubs. Drew even had her tenth birthday party inside the Limelight, a club in Manhattan. Even though there was cake, presents, and streamers that night, Drew just wanted a drink. As the year went on, Drew drank more and more. Sometimes, she even passed out from too much alcohol. Her acting skills allowed her to keep the truth from her mother, however.

Drew knew that she was different from other people her age. None of her classmates could go clubbing in downtown Los Angeles. Director Joel Schumacher, who later cast Drew in *2000 Malibu Road* and *Batman Forever,* remembers meeting and hanging out with Drew in the clubs. He told *Premiere* magazine, "Her

By the time she was ten, Drew had already begun the dangerous habit of drinking until she passed out.

mother, Jaid, was there all the time, and she brought Drew, who was [one of the only children] there. . . . I was . . . concerned about her being in a place like that at two or three in the morning. So we'd dance and we'd go to the balcony, let our legs dangle through the bars and watch everybody."[22]

Drew was beginning a dangerous pattern of drinking to excess and blacking out. She enjoyed the party life, and she was going out more and more. In just four short years she went from the sweet, unassuming little girl in *E.T.* to a jaded Hollywood child star. By the time she was eleven, Drew Barrymore saw her celebrity as a way to party rather than a way to further her career.

Chapter 3

In and out of Rehab

AFTER ONE NIGHT of heavy drinking at a club with her two friends, Drew rode home with one friend's mother. In the car, the mother took out a small pipe and began smoking pot. She offered the drug to the three girls. That night ten-year-old Drew got hooked on the effects of marijuana.

Partying was becoming more and more frequent for Drew while roles were few and far between. At eleven, she was at a difficult age for casting directors. She was too old to play the cute little girl, but she was also too young to play a teenager. Drew felt awkward as well. Her body was changing, and she was putting on weight. To make matters worse, she hid her addictions to drugs and alcohol from her mother, which caused her to become secretive and argumentative with Jaid.

Babes in Toyland

Both mother and daughter seemed relieved when Drew was finally cast in a television movie based on the book *Babes in Toyland*. Drew spent the summer of 1986, between her fifth- and sixth-grade year, filming in Munich, West Germany. Although she panicked at first, thinking she wouldn't have access to drugs and alcohol, Drew soon got used to working again and stayed nearly drug- and alcohol-free for almost four months. She was happy to be working, and she felt valued and appreciated, which helped her stay clean during the filming.

Drew fell in love for the first time that summer. Her boyfriend, a fifteen-year-old named Michael, worked on the film. The two spent much of their free time together, window shopping and dining out. Michael told Drew she was beautiful, and, for the first time, she believed it was true. But just like it had been with Jenny, their close relationship only made leaving difficult.

Once she was home, Drew went back to her old ways of drinking and doing drugs. She was feeling depressed, and after one particularly intense fight with her mother, Drew even contemplated committing suicide by taking a bottle of aspirin. Instead, she returned to numbing her pain with alcohol, cigarettes, and marijuana.

Drew was able to stay almost completely drug- and alcohol-free while she filmed the 1986 television movie Babes in Toyland *in West Germany.*

Drew also entered a new, exclusive preparatory school with students attending through grade twelve. Because she was used to spending time with adults, Drew befriended the older kids, identifying more with them than with students in her own class. "They [the older kids] smoked cigarettes and pot, ditched school, and generally had a poor attitude about anything that prevented them from having fun—which usually meant getting high,"[23] Drew says in her autobiography. Because her new friends could drive, Drew no longer relied on her mother for transportation. She could just be alone with her friends and come and go as she pleased.

The arrangement was perfect for Drew, who had begun to view her mother less as a parent and more as just the manager of her career; Jaid obviously wanted to help her daughter succeed, but she ignored many of the warning signs that Drew had other problems. "We're not the traditional mother-daughter scenario,"[24] Drew later admitted. Instead of being more inquisitive about her daughter's whereabouts or laying down strict rules, Jaid seemed preoccupied only with furthering Drew's career.

Drew, however, didn't seem to care about her career anymore. Although she had once looked forward to creating a new family on each set, she now saw any time away from her friends and their stashes of drugs and alcohol as too much to bear. So Drew was doubly upset when she learned that she had won a part in the film *See You in the Morning*. The drama, which explored the effects of divorce on a family, starred Jeff Bridges and Farrah Fawcett and was being filmed in New York. Not only would Drew be away from her friends, but she'd also be forced to spend all of her free time with her mother.

Downward Spiral

Because they spent so much time together on the set, Jaid finally began to notice Drew's abnormal and erratic behavior. Jaid had warned Drew off alcohol when she was nine, and she had simply assumed that her daughter had taken her advice. Jaid learned differently after Drew stumbled into their New York apartment at seven in the morning, sick from a night of excessive drinking. Jaid felt helpless, much as she had with Drew's father, and was driven

Drew Barrymore quickly realized that her fame could get her inside any nightclub she wished.

to tears after several fights with Drew, during which she learned of her daughter's secret life. Jaid tried grounding Drew, rationalizing with her, and even fighting to get her point across, but nothing seemed to work. Now thirteen, Drew wanted more freedom from her mother.

At the same time, Drew was learning that her fame helped her get into just about any club. And once she got inside, finding drugs was easy. The nightclubs teemed with people wanting to make some cash by selling drugs in the bathrooms, in dark corners, or sometimes even right out in the open.

Soon Drew found one drug she wanted more than any other: cocaine. The drug's effects were quick and clean. She never got sick like she did from drinking, and the effects of smoking pot often took a while to kick in. She usually found herself having to smoke more and more for the high it gave. Drew later explained,

> Alcohol made me feel horrible. It caused me to forget my pain, which is what I liked about it, but I always drank to excess and I woke up as sick as a dog, which I hated. Pot— that was fun for a while. Then I discovered cocaine, and it was like standing on top of a mountain and yelling, "Eureka! I found it!" Coke was the right drug for me. Neat and quick, with no apparent after-effect, coke allowed me to soar above my depression and sadness, above all my problems. What I couldn't see is that it eventually makes you go crazy.[25]

None of her films had been as successful as *E.T.*, and Drew was wondering if she'd ever lose the baby fat she saw standing in her way of the more grown-up, sexy roles she felt capable of playing. She first tried cocaine at a school dance and soon learned that doing the drug caused her to lose weight, which was good news to Drew since her next screen role, in the stalker film *Far from Home,* required her to wear a bikini. Cocaine was also a mood booster for Drew. What she didn't realize, however, was that the drug was more addictive than any other she'd tried—and she could never get enough.

Busted

Drew's late nights out became more the norm than the exception, and Jaid became increasingly conflicted about what to do about her daughter. One summer night, after partying with her usual group of older friends and missing her midnight curfew, Drew felt bold from the effects of alcohol. She called Jaid and demanded that her mother get out of the house and sleep somewhere else that night. Drew decided she didn't want to fight anymore, and since

Drew's late nights of partying increasingly became the norm rather than the exception.

her mother wouldn't leave her alone, Drew wanted her to leave. Amazingly, Jaid agreed.

With her mother gone, Drew seized the opportunity to stay out all night and consume as many beers as possible. She and her friends had beer races at the local drive-in movie theater, trying to consume as much alcohol in as little time as possible. As the evening wound down, an intoxicated Drew looked forward to going home, drinking more alcohol, and cranking up the stereo.

But when she went home, her mother's car was in the driveway. Furious, Drew began screaming at her mother and breaking anything that was in her path. A frightened Jaid knew this scene all too well. She had gone through something similar with Drew's father. But this time, she wasn't walking away—her daughter needed help. Jaid made a phone call to a friend whose daughter Chelsea had recently gone through drug and alcohol rehabilitation. Just a few hours later, Drew was admitted to the ASAP Family Treatment Center, a private rehab center in Van Nuys, California.

Getting Sober

Jaid had had enough of Drew's addictive, violent behavior. With the help of Drew's now-sober friend, Chelsea, and her mother, Jaid got Drew to the hospital. Sadly, she listened as Drew answered the orderly's questions about drugs she'd tried and how much alcohol she had consumed that night. Drew answered them truthfully, but she didn't understand that she was there for treatment. Like many addicts, she thought she had her alcohol and drug use under control and that her mother was just overreacting. She hoped to be out partying by nightfall.

However, Drew soon learned that her days and nights of partying were a thing of the past. Her first day at the center began with introductions to the counselors and an explanation of the strict rules at ASAP. Even though she was a celebrity, Drew was not treated any differently than any other patient. There were set times for meals, showers, and sleeping. She also had to attend individual and group therapy sessions as well as family therapy with Jaid.

However, after only twelve days, Jaid took her daughter out of treatment so that Drew could film the movie *Far from Home.* Jaid promised that Drew would be back in early September, and even though the counselors thought the time off was a bad idea, they issued a tech, or companion, to travel with the actress on location to Nevada. The tech, Diane, a former patient herself, would be a companion and confidante for Drew, helping to dissuade her from using drugs and making sure she stayed sober. At first, things went well. Drew felt pretty good about herself. She had lost some weight during her stay at the center, and the drugs and alcohol were no longer in her body.

Her good mood continued on the movie set. It wasn't easy, but she refrained from drinking and still accompanied the cast and crew to various local bars and casinos. She made it through the entire summer drug-free. But that seventy-eight-day sobriety streak would end abruptly on September 15, 1988.

Throwing It All Away

In early September, Drew had to return to New York to do some voice-over work for See You in the Morning and to audition for a play. Her doctors advised against her going, and Drew also had a feeling that something would go wrong. "I was real afraid something bad was going to happen to me,"[26] she recalls. The clubs in New York were especially tempting, but Drew reasoned that she had hung around people who drank and did drugs all summer. She naively thought she could have fun without being tempted.

One night at a club, though, the temptation proved too strong. At first, Drew just watched as some friends snorted lines of cocaine

Drew's Therapeutic Letter

Part of Drew's therapy at ASAP involved writing letters to friends and family, voicing her fears and frustrations. Often, these letters were never mailed or given to the people to whom they were addressed. Rather, the exercise was designed as a form of catharsis, a way to get out feelings and emotions by putting them on paper. During one session Drew was asked to write a letter to her father, which helped her deal with her feelings toward him. She quotes a portion of the letter in her autobiography, Little Girl Lost:

Dear Dad,

This is how I feel:

I feel like you were never there for me, and when you were there, it was only to hurt me. I really wish you would tell what you feel about me and tell me why. I never did anything but love you and keep forgiving you. And you never did anything but hurt me and cause me pain. Well, I'm all out of love and forgiveness for you. Love is a two-way street, and your street turned out to be a dead end.

If I had one wish it would be for you to straighten up and get your . . . act together. So many people have tried to help you, but all you've done [is ignore them]. I was like that too. Are you happy? Is that your wish? For your kids to be as messed up as you are.

I'll tell you one thing though. I'm going to get out of this and live a happy life, and unless you do a lot, you won't be part of that. I hope I'm wrong. I hope you will be a part of it. Somehow, I really would like to hear you say, "I love you, Drew." I really would.

But I guess I never will.

in the bathroom. They offered her some of the white powder and she refused. However, watching proved too much for Drew. She was emotionally fragile and even began to cry before she broke down and did some lines. Although she didn't want to blow her sobriety, she still craved the drug.

When she left the bathroom, Drew confessed to her friend Stacy that she'd blown her sobriety. By then, the drug's effects had taken hold, and Drew argued that since ASAP would know she'd done coke after they tested her urine (upon her return to the center), she might as well do some more. Even though Stacy tried to talk her out of it, Drew was determined to get her hands on more drugs. She convinced Stacy to party with her, and the two were out all night.

When they returned to Drew and Jaid's condo the next morning, Drew lied to her mother about where she'd been, claiming she'd slept at Stacy's. Jaid, convinced that Drew was still sober, believed her. She wanted to trust her daughter.

Lies and a Trip to L.A.

Drew, however, was using again and was ready for an adventure. She told her mother she was borrowing her credit card to return a clock she'd bought the day before. Instead, she and Stacy went to the airport and bought two tickets to Los Angeles and to Hawaii. Once they landed in California, the pair headed to Drew's house and began doing drugs. They did line after line of cocaine, bought clothes on the stolen credit card, and even smashed up Jaid's BMW. All the while, Drew was calling her mother, checking in, claiming she'd be home soon. But with each evasive phone call, Jaid got more and more suspicious. She hired private investigators to find Drew and take her back to the hospital.

Just hours before her flight to Hawaii was scheduled to leave, a coked-up Drew went into her bedroom to change her clothes and found two people standing in the room. They handcuffed her and drove her back to ASAP. There, Drew had to face all of the people who'd tried to help her the first time. She was ashamed and felt like she had let them all down by using drugs again. She explains in *Little Girl Lost,* "I ventured a quick glance at their faces

The ready availability of cocaine makes it easy for celebrities and others to begin or renew an addictive habit.

and they were looking at me with sadness in their eyes. It was the most severe punishment. Unable to bear their scrutiny, I bolted from the dining room, locked myself in the first empty dorm room I found, and prayed for a magic power that would allow me to disappear." [27]

Facing Her Fears

Drew couldn't disappear, though. Now that she was at ASAP, the counselors were even more determined to make sure that she finally straightened out. Although she tried to avoid them at first, she soon discovered that there was nowhere to hide. She was forced to admit she had hit bottom and was finally ready to recover. This method of letting patients realize that they have hit their lowest point and can now work on getting better is employed successfully by many recovery centers. "It was suddenly like opening a window on a gloomy day and letting in a ray of bright light,"[28] Drew says. The experience forced Drew to confront the things that depressed her—the ones that made her want to drink and do drugs. She had to work out her problems with her parents, overcome her fears, and deal with rules.

With the help of her counselors and doctors, Drew began a strict regimen of counseling and therapy to help her get well. She saw her mother only at family meetings. Jaid had been advised by the staff that this was best, yet at the same time, Drew also felt abandoned by her mother. Ultimately, Drew had good and bad days at ASAP, but her determination to get sober kept her on a path to recovery.

Growth Group

That determination to stay sober enabled Drew to follow the rules and respect figures of authority. This good behavior was rewarded with inclusion in Growth Group, a group that eased patients into the outside world again by allowing them to attend movies and concerts, visit parks, and go bowling or miniature golfing with former patients as chaperones.

Through Growth Group, Drew met Jan Dance, the wife of singer David Crosby. Crosby had known Drew's father when he was a young man, and Drew pumped him for information. Crosby and Drew talked about life, show business, and addiction over dinners and movies. She even got to watch some of the films that her father and grandfather had starred in many years ago. The relationship Drew forged with Dance and Crosby made her look forward to getting out of ASAP and starting over. Despite her growing impatience, however, the couple urged her not to rush it. "You'll know when it's time,"[29] Dance advised.

In Drew's mind, however, it was time. She had been at ASAP for nearly three months. Her relationship with her mother was getting better day by day. Both decided they would do whatever was needed to fix their relationship. They talked through their problems. Drew promised not to shut her mother out, and Jaid promised to put her role of mother over that of manager.

Drew had also come to terms with the fact that her father should not be a part of her life, a decision she made after a single

The relationship Drew Barrymore forged with Jan Dance and David Crosby helped her tremendously as she battled to overcome her addictions.

phone call. Jaid had given Drew John Barrymore's telephone number at his new home in New Mexico. Drew called and asked him how he was. At one point, the call got emotional. Drew told her dad that she loved him and he responded that he loved her, too. He then quickly asked for money. Drew denied his request and hung up the phone, feeling defeated and depressed. After that conversation, one of her friends at ASAP said that Drew shouldn't try to have a relationship with a father who doesn't want one with his child. Drew decided to take her friend's advice.

Severing the relationship with her father actually was good for Drew. She was happier than she had been in years. As time passed, Drew grew both excited and scared at the thought of leaving the center. She watched enviously as friends got their discharge dates. Finally, just a few days before Christmas, Drew learned she would be leaving ASAP. She had never felt a more conflicting series of emotions in her life. She was excited, nervous, petrified, and exhilarated. She prepared to be discharged by writing letters to her friends at ASAP and gathering her belongings. Finally, she was heading home.

Chapter 4

Getting Straight

M{ANY MEMBERS OF} the movie-going public wondered what had happened to the little girl from *E.T.* Some thought she was just in between child and adult roles, but few ever thought that she was recovering from years of drug and alcohol abuse. After so much struggle, Barrymore was ready to move on, get her life straightened out, and start working again, despite the public scrutiny she was about to face.

In the Public Eye

The day after Drew received her discharge date, she learned some bad news: The media had discovered that Drew Barrymore had undergone treatment for her problems, and they didn't want to leave the topic unresearched. Dealing with the media onslaught would be Drew's biggest challenge since getting sober.

Reporters showed up outside the center looking for a story, and hundreds of people called trying to find out if the rumor was true. Drew's mother and her friends at ASAP tried to hide the news from her. They believed that she was too emotionally fragile to handle what was going on and that the stress of such media scrutiny might drive her to drink or use drugs again. However, Drew, not yet fourteen years old, was stronger than anyone thought. She formulated a plan to tell her story, in her own words, to *People* magazine. She was determined to tell the story her way, reasoning that if the story were going to come out, it should at least be truthful.

In addition to the public attention, Drew had many adjustments to make upon leaving ASAP. She was dealing with people and situations that were new to her. Jan Dance and David Crosby helped her feel better about her reemergence into the world by giving her advice on "working the program." The ASAP program involved continued meetings and sponsorship from a fellow recovering addict and stressed taking one day at a time.

The plan made Barrymore feel stronger. She had ninety-six days of sobriety and was twenty-five pounds lighter than she had been when she entered ASAP. She managed to ignore the reporters who hung around outside her home and the endlessly ringing telephone. Drew relished being back at home and Christmas was especially happy for her that year. She was enjoying her freedom and simple things she'd missed while she was in the hospital, such as shopping and coming and going as she pleased. Yet there was still something missing. Drew wanted to get back to work.

Less than a week after she was released, Drew began filming an after-school special, *Fifteen and Getting Straight*, a story about teenage drug use. The special was filmed at ASAP, and Drew felt strange being there as an observer rather than as a patient. She compared it to returning to high school after having graduated. During the second week of filming, the January 16, 1989, issue of *People* hit newsstands with Drew's first-person account inside. Drew was relieved that her story was out and hoped the detail she

Drew Barrymore and actress Tatum O'Neal during filming of Fifteen and Getting Straight, *an after-school special about teenage drug use.*

had gone into would spare her from having to discuss her addiction and recovery at every interview.

The public's response to the story was overwhelmingly supportive. Letters flooded the *People* offices and more than 90 percent of them were positive. Several recovered addicts applauded Drew for being so open and candid. Others, however, couldn't believe that Jaid had allowed Drew to get away with as much as she had.

In the end, Drew's mother received a lot of criticism (justified or not) for the part she played in Drew's addiction. It was a result that neither Drew nor her mother had intended but that happened nonetheless. According to Jaid,

> That was to be expected. If people wanted to use me as the scapegoat, fine. It was Drew's decision to tell her story, and I was determined that it be *her* story, not mine. I blamed myself plenty and got over that. The real story is told in those multifamily groups we attended. You walk in thinking you're the worst parent on the planet, but then you see that kids and families from every possible situation are represented and you think, "My God, we've all ended up at the same point. It couldn't just be me." [30]

After the positive reaction to the story, Drew decided to stretch the article into an autobiography. That same year she began working with biographer Todd Gold on a book they later entitled *Little Girl Lost*.

Falling Off

However, just as the media seemed to be in Drew's corner, a *Star* tabloid story interrupted her good mood. Jaid had denied two *Star* reporters an interview, and they had claimed that she'd be sorry for denying them access to her daughter. The result was a blatant lie that left Drew fuming. The magazine claimed that Drew had fallen off the wagon by drinking at a Hollywood party. Although Drew knew the story was untrue, she wasn't sure how to handle it. She tried to ignore the lies, but she had to admit that temptation faced her every day. She knew that even though the story was false, something similar could happen one day if she weren't careful.

Drew knew she needed a new group of friends who didn't use drugs, but finding that group proved to be harder than she thought it would be. Furthermore, because she had spent so much time with older people, Drew was usually drawn to adults or teens at least a few years older than herself. This got her into trouble.

The night before her six-month anniversary of being sober, fourteen-year-old Drew was with her friend Andie, a seventeen-year-old party girl. As they drove around Los Angeles one night, Andie offered her some marijuana. Drew was torn and recalled thinking,

> [Smoking joints won't] blow my sobriety. I'm just looking to have fun. That's what I really believed. After all I'd been through, my twisted mind convinced itself without much difficulty than smoking dope was still nothing more than a brief amusement. But the bottom line was that I just wanted to get high. Nothing more, nothing less. I guess I missed it. My life at home wasn't so rough that I couldn't get along without it. I simply wanted to get high. No other reason.[31]

Later that night, while on their way home, Drew and Andie were in a car accident. A car traveling in the opposite direction crossed the highway median and slammed head-on into Andie's car. Drew hit the windshield and was knocked unconscious. When she came to, she called her mother to tell her what had happened. She didn't mention the drugs, however, pretending that she still had six months of sobriety.

Following the accident, Drew threw herself into doing well at school and in her career. She continued to attend AA (Alcoholics Anonymous) meetings and even began dating again. However, it was hard to erase the incident with Andie from her memory. It was also hard to forget how much she wanted the drugs.

Around the time she should have been celebrating eight months of sobriety, Drew slipped and got high with Andie again. This incident, however, proved even harder to live down. Although her first mistake could have been seen as a slipup, the second seemed to set a pattern, the start of using again. In retrospect, Drew admits she should have confessed to her mistakes instead of continuing to cover them up. She explains, "I was so scared of letting everyone else down that I embraced the lie more closely than ever. I had to, I convinced myself, for my own good. In reality, though, the lie wasn't for any of that. I lied to avoid letting down the one person who mattered most. Me."[32]

Perhaps due to her guilt and anger with herself, Drew and Jaid started fighting again with the same intensity they had before Drew had gotten treatment. Drew even ran away one morning. Luckily, David Crosby picked her up and brought her home with him. Although things seemed better at his house, even Crosby couldn't offer much help in repairing the relationship between mother and daughter. Drew knew something had to change at home.

An Almost-Fatal Mistake

That change came in the summer of 1989, when Drew moved out of Jaid's house and into a tiny West Hollywood apartment with her friend Edie. The teenager got a job as a door person at a nightclub three nights a week to help pay her bills. But being away from home wasn't easy. Drew fought with her roommate and had very little money. She was also still feeling guilty about her slipups. When her father called, asking for money, Drew turned him down, but rather than feel empowered by the decision, she lapsed into a spiral of depression.

When she called her mother for support, she learned that Jaid was planning a trip to New York and was taking one of Drew's former boyfriends with her to help move things out of the apartment she was selling there. Drew was hurt that her mother seemed content without her and angry that she seemed more interested in Drew's former boyfriend than in her own daughter. "All of a sudden, everything in my life seem to be piling up,"[33] Drew later wrote in her autobiography.

On July 4, 1989, things came to a head when Drew got into a huge argument with Edie. The fight was too much for Drew, and in a desperate attempt to show her friend just how serious and unhappy she really was, she picked up a knife from the kitchen counter. Drew remembers, "I made one very small scratch on my left wrist, then another, and in the heat of our back-and-forth argument, I made another. And that was the mistake. That third scratch. The knife slipped, I pressed too hard, and the blade sliced into my flesh."[34]

Drew passed out, and Edie and her boyfriend rushed her to the hospital. Drew asked to return to ASAP, for what would be her third stay there. This time, though, she was hoping that she would finally be healed. No one was any easier on Drew than they had been during her first two stays at ASAP. The difference was Drew's own attitude. This time, fourteen-year-old Drew knew she would leave the center healthy and sober and that she would stay that way.

She was also wise enough to realize that she needed help from her mother if her rehabilitation was going to last. She wanted her mother's support, and she hoped to repair their relationship. Between her former husband's and her daughter's addictions, however, coupled with her own denial and lack of parental authority, Jaid needed professional counseling, too. But she hadn't gotten any help other than family therapy at ASAP. Counselors at

Drew's problems increased until she checked herself into ASAP for the third and last time.

A Second Family

David Crosby understood Drew Barrymore's challenges and did whatever he could to help her overcome her addictions.

Like Drew, David Crosby led a wild life prior to getting sober. As a guitarist, he headed the 1970s rock group Crosby, Stills, Nash, and Young, known for songs such as "Teach Your Children," "Our House," and "Carry On." When he wasn't performing, however, the musician was abusing drugs. He battled a heroin addiction for more than twenty-five years before getting help. Once he had finally recovered, Crosby pursued a solo career and wrote his autobiography.

Crosby understood the pressures facing Drew perhaps better than most people. He knew what it felt like to be in the spotlight, fearful he'd be discovered if he slipped back into using drugs. He agreed to help Drew because he knew the obstacles she was up against and didn't want to see her destroy her life with drugs and alcohol.

Crosby and his wife, Jan Dance, introduced Drew to a sober but fun lifestyle. She befriended their friends and stayed away from bars and clubs. They welcomed her into their home like a daughter, and Drew has never forgotten their kindness. She remains close to both Crosby and Dance today.

ASAP recommended that Jaid check into a rehabilitation center called the Meadows in Wickenburg, Arizona. Just six hours after she was admitted, though, Jaid checked out, claiming that she was unable to handle the program's rigidity and the feeling that she was being incarcerated. Drew was livid. She told her mother, "This is not about you. This is about us! This is to get better so we can have a relationship."[35] Her daughter's desperate and angry words helped convince Jaid to return to the center.

Six weeks later, Drew visited her mother for the Meadows's family week, a time when families could visit and lend their support. Jaid and Drew were forced to confront each other with their feelings in a group session. Both were honest and open about how they felt. They seemed to come closer that week, and Drew returned to ASAP feeling like she and her mother had made real progress. Drew also had some revelations about herself. She says in her book, "I have to accept [myself], frailties and all, for who [I am], and not try to be someone else. I can't obsess about my weight. I can't compete with my mother. I can't find love where there isn't any love to be found. I can't go on beating myself up, emotionally or physically, or else I'll have the miserable life I've been trying so desperately to escape."[36]

By October 1989, Drew was ready to leave ASAP for the last time. Only this time, she decided to stay with David Crosby and Jan Dance instead of going home to Jaid. She loved her mother, but she thought their relationship might work better if they didn't live under the same roof. Her already good relationship with Dance and Crosby only got better during her stay there. She relied on them both and found a real father figure in Crosby. With the support of her mother, Dance, and Crosby, Drew finally felt like her life was on track and she was ready to move forward.

Back on Track

The release of her autobiography, *Little Girl Lost,* in 1990, made Drew feel like her past was truly behind her and she could start fresh. The book was incredibly popular and climbed to the top of best-seller lists. Drew's aspirations, however, were not as a writer. She was an actress who wanted to get back to the craft she loved. But before she made a move professionally, she knew that she had to straighten out her personal life and get a hold of her living situation.

Although she loved them, Drew couldn't continue living with Dance and Crosby; she didn't want to take advantage of their generosity. She didn't want to return home either, though, for fear that she would certainly argue with her mother. So Drew decided to follow the actions of Casey Brodsky, the character she'd played on-screen in *Irreconcilable Differences:* She divorced her parents. Drew followed California's Emancipation of Minors Law, which grants those under eighteen years of age independence from their parents, making them responsible and liable for their own actions. The law does not declare the parents incompetent but merely absolves them of all responsibility and liability for their children. Drew could marry, live alone, and establish her own credit. Recalling the day she won her independence, Drew says, "The judge said he couldn't turn back the clock, he could only turn it forward. I remember thinking, 'Thank God! I don't want to go back there!' I just knew: I am all of my responsibility. And I liked that feeling." [37]

After Drew won her case, she moved into her own apartment in Hollywood, dropped out of school, and got a job as a waitress at a coffee shop to make ends meet. Finally, fifteen-year-old Drew Barrymore was officially on her own and ready to form some semblance of a happy life.

Chapter 5

Back in the Spotlight

Drew Barrymore had her work cut out for her. Convincing Hollywood executives that she was healthy and ready to work again would not be easy. She was seen as too much of a financial risk. Films are bankrolled for millions of dollars by Hollywood studios, which need their stars to be stable and committed. Despite her name and reputation as a good actress, few people were willing to take their chances on her—at first.

Barrymore was forced to retreat back a few steps by taking small roles in even smaller films, and the blockbusters like *E.T.* seemed a long way off. Even so, she was happier than she'd been in a long while. She was committed to being sober, she was independent, and she was back doing what she loved.

The *Road* to Recovery

In 1992 Barrymore landed a leading role on *2000 Malibu Road,* a new CBS television series geared toward teens and young adults (similar in style to *Beverly Hills 90210* and *Melrose Place*). Barrymore played a character very different from herself—an innocent young girl trying to get a break in Hollywood. Barrymore decided she wanted to look different for the role, too, so she dyed her naturally light hair dark brown for the role. The show was popular during the summer of 1992, but it seemed to lose its audience as other networks began their new fall schedules. *2000 Malibu Road* lasted only one season, but Barrymore received good reviews for her role, and those reviews translated into more work.

The same year that she starred in *2000 Malibu Road,* Barrymore made four feature films (*Guncrazy, No Place to Hide, Motorama,* and *Poison Ivy*) and one made-for-television movie (*Sketch Artist*).

Working on *Guncrazy* reminded the actress why she loved her profession. The camaraderie on the set was nurturing, as the cast and crew got along like old friends. She later called her role in the film, that of Anita, a lonely high-schooler who begins corresponding with a prison inmate, one of the favorites of her career. (Her other favorite role was Gertie in *E.T.*) But Barrymore almost didn't land the role. Director Tamra Davis told *Premiere* magazine,

> I didn't want to meet her, because I didn't know she was interested in acting. I just knew her as, like, a trendy bad girl. And then she got a hold of me on the phone, and she said, "I've got to meet you. I *am* Anita." And so I met with her. And you know how Drew is—you're all in love with her. So I couldn't stop thinking about her. The producers were like, "Okay, we have to have blood tests [to make sure Drew was drug free] and give her rides to the set." And Drew was like, "No, you can trust me. Don't treat me like a baby." She took a stand and they let her do it.[38]

The cast, crew, and critics responded enthusiastically to Barrymore's work on the film. Vincent Canby, a film critic with the notoriously tough *New York Times,* claimed that she was set to become a major screen personality.

Drew Barrymore with Jennifer Beals (left) and Lisa Hartman (right), her costars on 2000 *Malibu Road. The short-lived series helped Barrymore revive her career.*

The Seductress

That course toward on-screen success continued as Barrymore played the lead role in the film *Poison Ivy*. Her character, Ivy, befriends a shy teen played by *Roseanne*'s Sara Gilbert and then seduces the girl's father. All the while, the man's wife is close to dying. The role was daring and was later singled out as Drew's comeback to the big screen.

The following year Barrymore played another seductress, a real-life character named Amy Fisher in the 1993 ABC made-for-television movie *The Amy Fisher Story*. Dubbed "the Long Island Lolita," sixteen-year-old Fisher made headlines in the early 1990s for trying to murder the wife of the much older man with whom she'd been having an affair. The ABC version of the story aired along with two other versions by competing networks, CBS and NBC. One starred television actress Alyssa Milano of *Who's the Boss* fame, and the other featured a young unknown in the leading role. Barrymore's version was undoubtedly the most well received of the three. Critics praised her performance, and the movie received the highest ratings of all three versions. Barrymore was back to doing what she did best—winning over audiences.

Dating and a Doomed Marriage

With her career back on track, Barrymore's good mood was contagious. She was attracting many would-be boyfriends. One of them was aspiring actor and musician Jamie Walters, perhaps best-known for playing Ray Pruitt on the long-running series *Beverly Hills 90210*. The two became serious fairly quickly. Barrymore even got a tattoo bearing Jamie's name on her back. She added it to her collection, which includes butterflies on her stomach and a cross with vines on her ankle. The couple dated for a year and even became engaged before the relationship ended.

Ever the romantic, though, Barrymore kept dating. One day, in March 1994, those romantic ideals almost got her into trouble when she suddenly married her boyfriend of just six weeks. Having steered clear of the tabloids for several years, her face was back on the cover of many magazines. Her groom was Jeremy Thomas, a thirty-one-year-old Welshman who ran a bar in Los Angeles.

Barrymore dated actor and musician Jamie Walters for a year.

Barrymore says she truly believed that Thomas was the love of her life. She agreed to the marriage for this reason and because Thomas needed a green card. If Barrymore, a U.S. citizen, married him, he would be allowed to stay in the country permanently.

On March 20, 1994, at 5:00 A.M., nineteen-year-old Barrymore stood before a minister in Thomas's bar. The couple had decided to marry at the spur of the moment, calling the minister in the middle of the night and asking him to perform the ceremony. Just seven weeks later, though, Barrymore realized that she'd made a mistake and filed for divorce. Thomas, it turned out, had been interested only in getting his green card and had little regard for Barrymore or her feelings. "It's the only thing I've done in my life that was untruthful to myself," Barrymore later admitted to a *Harper's Bazaar* reporter in 1996. "It's really ruined marriage for me."[39]

Boys on the Side

Barrymore's next film, *Boys on the Side* was released in early 1995, just after her divorce was finalized. In the movie, she plays a wild girl who realizes she doesn't need a man to be happy. Right after she does, however, her pregnant character meets the man she

Barrymore on Relationships

Relationships—whether platonic friendships or romances—make Barrymore happy. She claims that since people can't pick their families, they can have some control over the relationships they choose. Barrymore relates more in the January 1999 issue of *Teen* magazine.

> My friendships are the only relationships I've ever known. I have the greatest respect for them. They've been a tremendous influence on my life and helped me figure out who I am. I think friends make your dreams come true. . . . I do believe in love at first sight. But I also believe in "How do you keep it going? How do you keep a consistent, healthy relationship that's communicative and has compromise, yet allows you to remain the individual [whom the person] fell in love with?"

wants to marry. Buoyed by big names like Barrymore, Whoopi Goldberg, and Mary-Louise Parker, and coupled with a strong, moving script, *Boys on the Side* was a hit with both critics and audiences. Barrymore also seemed to accept the title as her own personal mantra for dating. At that point in her life, her career was at the forefront and boyfriends were secondary.

Flower Films Blooms

With her career as her priority, Barrymore decided to start her own production company, which she named Flower Films. Barrymore formed the company in 1994, for two reasons: to help her own career as an actor, and to help the careers of other actors as a producer. Barrymore decided that she wanted the power to help create a movie from start to finish, from conception of an idea to marketing it to the public. "I wanted to produce because I know that work, no matter what job you're in, can be done with respect," she told *Teen People* magazine in 1999. "It doesn't have to be competitive or political. This is an opportunity to make that happen."[40]

When it came time to find a business partner, Barrymore remembered a woman she'd met in Seattle, Washington, named Nancy Juvonen. Even though the two had, at first, talked for just a few hours, Juvonen was just the kind of partner Barrymore knew she wanted. Taking a chance, Barrymore called twenty-seven-year-old Juvonen and asked her to be her business partner. "She called me and said, 'I dare you to come to Los Angeles and work with me,'"

Juvonen recalled to *Seventeen* magazine. "We clicked in a business sense. She's unique and I'm immature. I thrive on systems and organization, while Drew is so creative. A lot of the businessy stuff doesn't interest her, so we both enjoy doing what we excel at."[41]

Next, the two hired four female assistants to read scripts and help choose projects for Barrymore to star in as well as to acquire scripts for the company to produce. Barrymore had a pretty good idea of what she wanted to accomplish through Flower Films. She wanted to lighten up the world of movies. She told *InStyle* magazine in 1999, "As an actor I'll want to continue to do darker characters. But the only movies I want to produce for people are fun, caper, funny, romance movies—all the good stuff in life."[42]

To that end, Barrymore signed a deal with Fox Pictures 2000 to produce several films. The first film that Flower Films was in charge of, the goofy, romantic comedy *Never Been Kissed,* starred Barrymore and premiered in the spring of 1999. Since then, Barrymore's company has produced another film, *Charlie's Angels,* in which she also starred. She remains awed and excited about her role behind the camera. She told *Teen People,* "I can't believe I can get a movie made. It's the oddest thing in the world and yet, I can do it."[43]

In Front of the Camera

Despite her interests as a producer, Barrymore still wanted to act. Her previous successes gave her a wider variety of roles from which to choose. In the 1995 film *Mad Love,* for example, she played a girl she understood pretty well. Her character, a troubled teenage girl named Casey, is manic-depressive and suicidal. (Barrymore understood depression and had entertained the thought of suicide on more than one occasion.) Playing the character was rewarding for Barrymore, but she realized she didn't need to be the star of a film to feel worthwhile.

Although she had been a star since she was seven, Barrymore wasn't above making small cameo appearances in films she liked. During the early 1990s she appeared on-screen for just a few minutes in the comedy *Wayne's World 2,* and in *Batman Forever* she played Sugar, the ultra-evil, ultra-feminine sidekick to Tommy Lee Jones's Two-Face. Then, in 1996, the actress fooled audiences when she took a small role in the teen slasher flick *Scream*. Although she was featured in posters and ads promoting the film, Barrymore's character was killed in the first scene, turning over the movie to lesser-known actors. The film did incredibly well, spawning two sequels, the last of which Barrymore also produced without the backing of Flower Films.

Around the time *Scream* was released, twenty-one-year-old Barrymore was ready for a change in the movies she made. In just a few years she'd starred as a teenage vixen, a manic-depressive, and a murder victim. When she heard that renowned director Woody Allen was casting for his new musical film *Everyone Says I Love You*, she was determined to land a role even though she couldn't sing. Allen cast her as Skylar, the daughter of leads Alan Alda and Goldie Hawn, and dubbed, or had someone else sing, Barrymore's one song, a duet with actor Edward Norton, who played her fiancé. Working with Allen turned out to be just as rewarding as Barrymore had imagined, and the two show-business veterans became fast friends. She also befriended Hawn and Norton. Norton even shared an apartment with Barrymore in New York's West Village after filming ended.

Drew Barrymore waves to the crowd as she arrives for the premiere of Scream.

Return of the Wild Child

Even after she stopped drinking and using drugs, Drew Barrymore still ran a little wild. In 1994 she made headlines for flashing late-night talk-show host David Letterman while she danced on his desk. In early 1995 Barrymore revealed even more by posing for *Playboy* magazine. Her godfather, Steven Spielberg, had his special effects team draw clothes over the published pictures, which he sent to Drew as a joke with a note telling her to cover up.

These experiences were not without lessons, however. Barrymore has said she learned that she doesn't need to reveal too much of herself anymore. "I'm not going to take my clothes off anymore. I don't do wild things anymore," she told *People* magazine in the May 12, 1997, 50 Most Beautiful People issue.

Still, after years of feeling like an ugly duckling, Barrymore is now happy with how she looks and her weight: "I've never looked in the mirror and said, 'You look so hot!' But it's important to feel good about yourself. . . . I finally realized that I don't have to have an A-plus perfect body, and now I'm very happy the way I am." Others are happy with the way Barrymore looks as well. She was named one of *People* magazine's fifty most beautiful people in 1997.

Even though she no longer drinks or uses drugs, Barrymore still has a reputation for being a little wild.

Drew stayed in New York City to film her next movie, *Wishful Thinking*. However, even though she loved Manhattan, she was not very happy with the film. Making *Wishful Thinking*, though, was part of a deal Barrymore worked out with Miramax Films. In exchange for the chance to work on *Everyone Says I Love You*, she had to make *Wishful Thinking*. It was an arrangement the actress didn't like. She revealed to *Harper's Bazaar* in 1996,

I was really unhappy on that movie [*Wishful Thinking*], be-cause I got manipulated into doing it. Gwyneth Paltrow had the same deal with Miramax and had to make *The Pallbearer* [a film that did not do well] to get *Emma* [the movie that made Paltrow a star]. And it's so funny, because she totally busted Harvey Weinstein [co-chairman of Miramax] in an interview. So I'm like, not only hats off to Gwyneth Paltrow but I'm gonna do it, too! I got . . . ma-nipulated into doing a . . . movie I hated![44]

In the end, the experience taught Barrymore a lesson. She vowed to do things on her own terms from then on and never again be manipulated into doing work she disliked.

Romantic Comedienne

Barrymore's next film, the romantic comedy *Home Fries,* was one she wholeheartedly wanted to make. It was a long-awaited chance to work with her boyfriend, actor Luke Wilson, whom she'd met in 1996. Although she had briefly dated several men since the end of her marriage, she was serious about Wilson. The two even talked about getting married before they broke up in 1998.

For her role as a pregnant fast-food worker, Drew padded her stomach and worked on her Southern accent. She also dyed her hair red. Although the film wasn't a hit in theaters, Barrymore was happy on the set and pleased with the finished product.

The director, Dean Parisot, however, worried whether the movie would be a success. He feared that Wilson and Barrymore's relationship wasn't going to last through the filming. He explains to *People Weekly,* "I'm pretty sure I heard them having their first ar-gument. I was like, 'Oh, my God, they're breaking up right before [filming the movie's] big love scene."[45] The two didn't split then. In fact, they just got closer, a pleasant surprise for Parisot and a fact that proved to strengthen the characters' relationship on film.

Barrymore's next film provided the critical and financial suc-cess that *Home Fries* lacked. *The Wedding Singer,* starring funnyman Adam Sandler, was a comedy set in the year 1985. Adam Sandler's character, Robbie Hart, falls in love with a banquet waitress (played by Barrymore), even though she's engaged to a successful

Wall Street trader. The film featured plenty of 1980s tunes and jokes, which led critic Leah Rozen of *People Weekly* to say, "If you're clueless as to who or what any of these cultural touchstones are, you'll miss half the film."[46] Most people did get the cultural references, and *The Wedding Singer* became one of Barrymore's most successful films.

Josie Grossy

While she was filming *The Wedding Singer*, Barrymore heard a storyline for another comedy. As her partner, Nancy Juvonen, tells *Teen People,* "I pitched her the story one night when all of *The Wedding Singer* guys were over at my house. I was too excited to wait. The next day, Drew came into my office and said, 'I read it. I love it. Let's do it!'"[47]

The movie was *Never Been Kissed,* and its plot revolves around a twenty-five-year-old copy editor named Josie who gets a unique assignment from the newspaper she works for: to go back to high

Drew Barrymore starred as Adam Sandler's love interest in the popular romantic comedy The Wedding Singer.

Barrymore relived some of the awkwardness she felt as a grade-school student during the filming of Never Been Kissed.

school as an undercover student. The task is both exhilarating and scary for Josie, who was a geek in high school and whose nickname was Josie Grossy.

As both star and producer, Barrymore had her hands full with *Never Been Kissed*. She didn't mind the work, though, because making the movie was a real labor of love for the actress. The unattractive, unpopular Josie was a character Barrymore understood well. She told *Teen People* in May 1999,

> I love playing [Josie] because I relate to her more when she is in "Grossy" mode. . . . When she's more attractive [later in the film], I almost feel less comfortable in her skin. I feel like I'm so more in touch with what it's like to feel awkward. I can understand that feeling. I related to the script so much. I wanted to talk about, for one, feeling good about who you are and embracing that. A person's looks are never going to make you love them or like them.[48]

Even though she never attended high school, she felt she could identify with what Josie was going through because her own earlier school years had been very similar. "It was awful. People wouldn't even talk to me. I think they assumed I must be a jerk if I'm an actor. I believe they just made an assumption and didn't want to take the time to figure out if it wasn't true. I don't harbor any resentment about that, but it was a lonely experience,"[49] Drew later admitted to *Teen* magazine.

For the film, Barrymore assembled a cast of relative newcomers. The list included Jessica Alba, Marley Shelton, and Michael Vartan, who played the teacher upon whom Josie develops a crush. Vartan was especially grateful for Barrymore's guidance and trust in his abilities. He tells *Teen People,* "She's one of the main reasons that I got this part. I heard through the grapevine that she really fought to get me in this film. To a studio, I'm still a nobody, so this is a great opportunity. It's funny how when nice people are at the head of something, it sort of trickles down."[50] When they weren't filming, the cast members became like a family, even competing against one another in games of Yahtzee.

The experience of making *Never Been Kissed* made Barrymore even more determined to continue producing as well as acting. "The work was so . . . much fun. It was so great. It takes up every second of your time and you never get upset for a second. In fact, you're like, 'More, more—more hours in the day!' "[51] she recalls.

With her schedule full, Barrymore looked forward to each day. She was always grateful for the opportunity to work, and that was just what she planned to continue doing.

Chapter 6

Hollywood's Princess

A<small>T THE START</small> of the twenty-first century, Drew Barrymore took her place in the long line of famous Barrymore actors. She had also finally figured out how to take the best of her family legacy and leave behind the curse of addiction. By the late 1990s she had become one of the most successful young actresses in the business. Instead of convincing movie companies to hire her, she was in charge of her own films and was being offered dozens of roles a year.

A Real-Life Cinderella

In 1998 Barrymore became a princess on-screen when she brought the fairy tale *Cinderella* to life in the movie *Ever After*. Barrymore and the rest of the cast and crew, including legendary actress Angelica Huston, traveled to an isolated village in France to film the classic tale of a young woman who marries a prince. Despite the fact that the story takes place in the sixteenth century, screenwriters put a feminist spin on it. *Ever After* focuses less on fantasy and more on establishing Cinderella as intelligent and considerate. The new spin on the story was creative, and both fans and critics alike were impressed by the new version of a well-known tale. *People Weekly* explains in its review,

> The prince, for example, first meets Cinderella while on the run from an arranged marriage to a Spanish princess. The orphaned Cinderella remains with her stepmother because she keeps hoping the woman will actually express maternal feeling for her. And Cinderella's fairy godmother is—hold on to your paintbrush—Leonardo da Vinci, who is hanging about doing some artwork for the prince's father.[52]

While making *Ever After,* Barrymore charmed everyone on the set. Because she's a vegetarian, she brought nonmeat alternatives to the catering table, including fresh fruit and veggie sandwiches that she both prepared and had catered. Dougray Scott, who played the prince, claims, "She's one of the most generous people I've ever met."[53] The movie was embraced by critics and audiences in 1998. *People Weekly* even called the film "one of the unexpected delights of the summer." Its reviewers had especially high praise for Barrymore's work in the film, saying, "Barrymore is delectable, switching back and forth between fierce displays of temper and blushing uncertainty."[54] Barrymore was even nominated for a Blockbuster Entertainment Award for the role.

Barrymore's Castle

Every Hollywood princess needs a castle, and Barrymore found hers nestled in the hills above Los Angeles. Although a far cry from the French château she occupied while filming *Ever After,* the house is spacious and has its own luxuries. The solar-heated, recycled-cedar barn was built in 1902, and the property encompasses two and a half acres in the Coldwater Canyon section of the city.

Drew Barrymore and Dougray Scott in Ever After. *The film told the story of Cinderella with a feminist twist.*

As soon as she moved in, Barrymore added her own unique touches to the spacious house. She built a Polynesian tiki bar, complete with a thatched roof and its own patch of sand, to give her guests the feeling of being on the beach. She also converted one of the house's many bedrooms into a yoga studio designed by a student of famous architect Frank Lloyd Wright. The house also features a guest cottage, swimming pool, a chicken coop, a beehive, and plenty of room for her two dogs, Flossie and Templeton, to play. Barrymore's favorite room in the house, though, is her library, where she houses her collection of rare first-edition books.

Once she had settled into her new home, Barrymore did something she never thought she would do: She invited her homeless father to stay in the apartment over her garage. After years of bitterness, Drew and John Barrymore finally made amends. Although she doesn't go into the details of their reconciliation, the younger Barrymore is happy that they're close. As she tells *InStyle* magazine, "[My dad] is so great, but he's wild. I didn't want to be like him, the way he was always struggling and never had a place to live. I want to know where I'm going. That stability is important to me." [55]

Barrymore's relationship with her mother, however, hasn't improved. They have spoken only twice in eight years. She's still not sure what went wrong between them. She says, "It's because . . . I don't know. I don't understand her. And I tried to for so long. I just think that too much . . . has happened. . . . I think we differ in the fact that she seems to love [the] Hollywood [lifestyle] and I hate [the] Hollywood [lifestyle]." [56]

Alone and Happy

With her new home and flourishing career, Barrymore's life seemed perfect. But after two years, she and actor Luke Wilson parted ways in late 1998. She took a Hawaiian vacation to clear her head after the breakup, which she claimed was amicable.

In the months that followed, Barrymore spent time with her friends and enjoyed being alone. For the first time since she was a young teenager, Barrymore knew she would be okay without a boyfriend. The realization was welcomed and liberating: She had enough love from other sources to compensate for the romantic love she had always thought she needed. As she explains in *Teen People,* "Sometimes it's strange because I don't have love in my life—in the boyfriend sense. But I have it from other places, and hopefully, always from myself. I no longer have the fear of being alone, because I am alone, and it's not scary. It's cool to find out that you don't need a boyfriend to be happy."[57]

Meeting Tom Green

In the fall of 1999, though, Barrymore met Canadian comic and actor Tom Green. At first, their relationship was strictly professional. Barrymore asked Green if he would take a small part in *Charlie's Angels,* a film she was both starring in and producing. Green explains, "She said she was a fan. We met once and talked a couple of times on the phone about the part. Then I didn't see her until we shot the thing [in January 2000]."[58] The two met for coffee and had lunch while filming, and the chemistry between them was evident. Not long after, they became a couple.

However, the relationship almost ended before it even began. Green was diagnosed with testicular cancer on March 9, 2000, just six weeks after he and Barrymore began dating. Green expected Barrymore to break off the relationship because his situation was so serious and they were a new couple. But she surprised him by sticking by his side. Green underwent surgery to remove the cancer, and Barrymore stayed in the hospital with him, sleeping in his room and constantly offering support. A friend of Green's tells *US Weekly,* "She was remarkable. Her spirit was so vital to how Tom got through the ordeal."[59] Barrymore's admiration, however, was reserved for twenty-nine-year-old Green. She says, "He's been so brave."[60]

After Green recovered, the relationship grew even more serious. By July 2000 the two had become engaged. At first, news of the engagement was met with skepticism in the media; Green was known for his practical jokes. But publicists for both actors confirmed the rumor. The couple was then spotted at a Hollywood premiere that summer, and Barrymore had a large, glittering diamond on her left hand.

Even though they'd been together only a short while, Barrymore had her suspicions that Green was going to propose on the

Drew's support of her boyfriend, comedian Tom Green, during his bout with cancer was remarkable.

day he did. "The minute we woke up that day, something inside told me that Tom was going to propose. I said yes immediately. It's going to be a blast, romantic and full of jokes,"[61] Barrymore says of their nuptials.

She is equally enthusiastic about the man she plans to marry. She told *InStyle* magazine in September 2000, "I have the best fiancé that ever lived. He's so romantic, a wonderful gentleman, an incredible listener. He's not just the [wacky characters] you see on the [*Tom Green Show* on MTV]."[62]

Barrymore seems to have found her Prince Charming. As she explained to *InStyle* in March 1999, she had always imagined how she would know that she had found her ideal mate: "I've always said that one night I'm going to find myself in some field somewhere. I'm standing on grass, and it's raining, and I'm with the person I love, and I know I'm at the very point I've been dreaming of getting to. Life just happens in moments. I believe that."[63]

Yet even though she cherishes those moments with Green and is excited to marry and begin a life with him, Barrymore's also got

Jaid Cashes In

For years, Jaid Barrymore has insisted that she isn't riding on the coattails of her daughter's fame, yet many of her actions prove she might be doing just that. In September 1995 she posed for *Playboy* magazine, just nine months after her daughter did. And currently, she's working on a book called *Confidential*, in which she plans to reveal in-depth descriptions of her romantic affairs with many of Hollywood's leading men.

But perhaps most upsetting to Drew Barrymore was an auction that her mother tried to organize on the Internet in November 1999. Jaid planned to auction off eighteen of her daughter's personal items, including the little red cowboy hat Barrymore wore in *E.T.*; the hat had a starting price of $45,900. The online auction closed after just ten days, though, because none of the items got their minimum bids. Barrymore was reportedly upset that her mother was trying to cash in by selling her childhood memories.

The red cowboy hat Drew wore in E.T. is just one item her mother tried to sell in an online auction.

her feet on the ground. She told *Premiere* magazine in November 2000, "I'm excited to create this wonderful family, and to do it with someone who will be laughing with me through it all. Tom and I have been through some intense stuff already together, so I don't approach this like a fantasy. This is the first time I've actually had a hold on a reality that I've always dreamed of. It feels very real."[64]

An Angelic Role

In February 1999 Barrymore got the go-ahead to do a movie version of the 1970s television series *Charlie's Angels*. She had long been a fan of the show, but she wanted to make some changes in the big-screen version. She and Juvonen decided that the three Angels wouldn't carry guns, like they did on the television show. Barrymore explains to *Teen People*, "Guns are cowardly. With the flick of one finger, you can kill somebody. I always think about what the world would be like if people didn't have that ability."[65] Instead, the movie's premise is that the characters are martial-arts experts.

Barrymore signed on as star and producer, and the project was intense from the start. Actress Cameron Diaz (perhaps best known for *There's Something About Mary*) signed on right away to play the second Angel, but the film was still one shy of the required three; the original series starred Farrah Fawcett, Kate Jackson, and Jaclyn Smith as the original Angels.

While they searched for the third actress, Barrymore and Diaz met five hours a day with the script creators to come up with plot lines and develop their characters. They also began intense training with a kung fu master. "We were so sore after the first few sessions, that we went to Cameron's house and took a bath in Epsom salt and cried,"[66] Barrymore admits to *Teen People*.

According to reporters, sore muscles were only part of the problems on the set. The stars and producers, however, deny claims that there were many arguments between the actors. "The studio [Sony] gave us a big budget, so immediately that garners negative press,"[67] Juvonen explains in *Seventeen* magazine. Despite such statements, there were rumors of vicious fights and differences between the third Angel cast, Lucy Liu, and actor Bill Murray. Screenwriters were also having trouble coming up with a final script.

The rumors made Barrymore mad. She was close enough to the project to feel as though people were attacking her, her cast, and her crew. Furthermore, she tells *US Weekly,* making the movie had become tremendously important to the cast and crew: "We're here every day—and of course it's not just a movie to us! We're obsessed! We're totally narrow-minded! It's all we do!"[68]

Charlie's Angels became so much a part of Barrymore's life for most of 1999 and early 2000 that she wasn't sure what she was going to do when it was over. Her friendships with Liu and Diaz had become so tight, that they dreaded not seeing one another every day. When filming was complete, to say good-bye, Barrymore invited more than one thousand people to her house for the wrap party to celebrate. She laid out canvases and paints, set up four bars, created a game room with air hockey, and even set up a screening room where old episodes of the *Charlie's Angels* television series played.

Barrymore and her Charlie's Angels *costars Lucy Liu (left) and Cameron Diaz (center).*

The Queen of Comedy

One event, however, did take Barrymore away from shooting *Charlie's Angels*. In January 2000 she learned that she would be the recipient of ShoWest's Comedy Star of the Year Award. ShoWest, an annual presentation of the National Association of Theater Owners, gives awards based on audience appeal and box-office receipts. Barrymore was the first woman recognized by the organization in the comedy category. She traveled to Las Vegas, Nevada, in early March to accept the prestigious award. While there, she announced some upcoming projects, including an adaptation of Robert Nathan's novel *So Love Returns,* which she plans to star in and produce. She also discussed her role of being the voice for a character in Twentieth Century Fox's *Titan A.E.,* an animated science fiction film that was released in the summer of 2000.

The ShoWest award wasn't the first time Barrymore had been singled out for her comedic gifts. She had also been nominated for an American Comedy Award for *The Wedding Singer,* and she had won a Blockbuster Entertainment Award in 1999. Barrymore is always honored by the recognition and is humble when she accepts her awards. She's simply happy to be working and plans to continue to do so into old age. As she explained to *Premiere* magazine in November 2000,

> I would really love that [working until she's old], but if that doesn't happen, that's okay, too. Because of the way my career was, I always think every job is my last. With everything that happened, people didn't know if I was stable enough to work. . . . And then the transition that child actors have to make into adulthood—those two elements combined make me feel like I'm never going to work again after each movie.[69]

Helping Those Less Fortunate

In addition to being busy making movies and winning awards, Barrymore donates what time she can to charity. She's a spokeswoman for the Female Health Foundation, visiting college campuses and talking with women about sexually transmitted diseases. She also helps raise funds for Wildlife Waystation, a rescue or-

Barrymore donates her time to various charitable causes, including Wildlife Waystation, a rescue organization for wild animals.

ganization for wild animals. Barrymore has always spoken out for animal rights, and her love of animals led her to become a vegan, swearing off meat and animal by-products. She's also donated her time to fight pediatric AIDS. But, according to her partner, Nancy Juvonen, Barrymore always wants to do more. Juvonen tells *Seventeen* magazine,

I think that she has many demands on her as an actress, producer, and philanthropist. But maybe the really tough thing is when she gets that letter from the person in the Midwest who's staging a fund-raiser at her or his school for the kid who has to have the liver transplant. Those [kinds of] requests come in by the bucketloads. There are so many events where Drew would just show up at the small auditorium, and they'd raise thousands of dollars. It's difficult to turn people down, but she can't always help.[70]

Barrymore's desire to help others is often in conflict with her desire to work at a furious pace. There just aren't enough hours in the day to devote the kind of time she'd like to each. Her attitude, however, inspires her costars and friends, such as Edward Norton, who says, "[Barrymore] is one of the few people I know who has a sincere and self-motivated desire to give energy back to other people."[71]

Putting It All in Perspective

Drew Barrymore has lived a very full life, and she plans to continue doing so. She doesn't regret anything in her past. Instead, she realizes that everything that has happened to her—including all of the mistakes she's made—has led her to where and who she is now. She's at peace with her stardom, saying in May 2000, "I'm lucky. I grew up being famous, so I don't have any weird things about be-

Barrymore's Plan

In November 2000 reporter Sean M. Smith of *Premiere* magazine asked Drew Barrymore if she had a life plan. She responded to his question in the article "A Whole New Drew."

I have *plans*. I don't have *a* plan. I would like to have a family and live [in] different places, and yet always have a base. I would like to give myself time to do something else other than work. I want to take all these things that I've learned, knowing it was all accumulated for my kids, and be completely open to a world of real learning. I would like to enable more filmmakers to make their movies. I really would like to direct. I'm not going to talk about it. I have to go do it. I'm not ready yet. Read more books. I just want to rock the show, you know?

ing famous. I imagine it must be harder if fame hits you in the middle of your life. I wouldn't know how someone handles that."[72]

Many people wonder how Barrymore managed to handle the hardships in her life. She was the victim of hereditary drug and alcohol abuse and the product of a dysfunctional single-parent home. Today, though, she is a highly successful producer and actress and has remained honest and humble, eager just to do good work.

Drew Barrymore wants to continue doing what she loves—performing and producing, loving and laughing. However, even bubbly Barrymore sometimes gets run-down. She admits to having gone through what she calls a midlife crisis at age twenty-four. After twenty-three years of working, she considered giving it all up, retiring, and disappearing. The crisis didn't last long, though. Such depression isn't part of her life anymore. She says, "I thought, That's crazy: I can't retire—I've got too much time to go. And I couldn't sit still if I tried."[73]

Notes

Introduction: Living Up to a Legacy

1. Drew Barrymore with Todd Gold, *Little Girl Lost*. New York: Simon & Schuster, 1990, p. x.
2. Barrymore, *Little Girl Lost*, p. x.
3. Quoted in Jonathan van Meterm, "Drew on Top," *Harper's Bazaar,* December 1996, p. 181.
4. Quoted in *People Weekly,* "Young and Hot: Top 10 Players Under 35," November 18, 1996, p. 62.

Chapter 1: A Star Is Born

5. Quoted in Sarah Saffian, "Pistol-Packin' Mama," *US Weekly,* June 5, 2000, p. 62.
6. Barrymore, *Little Girl Lost,* p. 33.
7. Barrymore, *Little Girl Lost,* p. 43.
8. Barrymore, *Little Girl Lost,* p. 41.
9. Quoted in Trish Dietch Rohrer, "True Drew," *InStyle,* November 2000, p. 566.

Chapter 2: The Life of a Celebrity

10. Barrymore, *Little Girl Lost,* p. 54.
11. Barrymore, *Little Girl Lost,* p. 56.
12. Barrymore, *Little Girl Lost,* p. 67.
13. Barrymore, *Little Girl Lost,* p. 68.
14. Barrymore, *Little Girl Lost,* p. 70.
15. Barrymore, *Little Girl Lost,* pp. 77–78.
16. Barrymore, *Little Girl Lost,* p. 85.
17. Barrymore, *Little Girl Lost,* p. 90.
18. Barrymore, *Little Girl Lost,* p. 93.

19. Barrymore, *Little Girl Lost*, p. 94.
20. Barrymore, *Little Girl Lost*, p. 95.
21. Barrymore, *Little Girl Lost*, p. 101.
22. Quoted in Holly Millea, "Drew's Rules," *Premiere*, September 1998, p. 100.

Chapter 3: In and out of Rehab

23. Barrymore, *Little Girl Lost*, p. 130.
24. Quoted in Millea, "Drew's Rules," p. 101.
25. Barrymore, *Little Girl Lost*, p. 153.
26. Barrymore, *Little Girl Lost*, p. 191.
27. Barrymore, *Little Girl Lost*, p. 205.
28. Barrymore, *Little Girl Lost*, p. 207.
29. Quoted in Barrymore, *Little Girl Lost*, p. 249.

Chapter 4: Getting Straight

30. Quoted in Barrymore, *Little Girl Lost*, p. 265.
31. Barrymore, *Little Girl Lost*, p. 274.
32. Barrymore, *Little Girl Lost*, pp. 279–80.
33. Barrymore, *Little Girl Lost*, p. 290.
34. Barrymore, *Little Girl Lost*, p. 291.
35. Barrymore, *Little Girl Lost*, p. 296.
36. Barrymore, *Little Girl Lost*, p. 302.
37. Quoted in Saffian, "Pistol-Packin' Mama," p. 62.

Chapter 5: Back in the Spotlight

38. Quoted in Millea, "Drew's Rules," p. 87.
39. Quoted in van Meterm, "Drew on Top," p. 183.
40. Quoted in Amy Brooks, "Never Been Better," *Teen People*, May 1999, p. 51.
41. Quoted in Geri Sahn and Michele Shapiro, "You Know It's Drew," *Seventeen*, October 2000, pp. 140, 141.
42. Quoted in Trish Deitch Rohrer, "True Drew," *InStyle*, March 1999, p. 294.
43. Quoted in *Teen People*, "25 Hottest Stars Under 25," March 2000, p. 43.
44. Quoted in van Meterm, "Drew on Top," p. 184.
45. Quoted in Kyle Smith and Julie Jordan, "In *Home Fries* and

at Home, Luke Wilson Sizzles with Drew Barrymore," *People Weekly,* December 7, 1998, p. 139.

46. Quoted in Leah Rozen, "*The Wedding Singer,*" *People Weekly,* February 16, 1998, p. 19.

47. Quoted in Brooks, "Never Been Better," p. 51.

48. Quoted in Brooks, "Never Been Better," p. 51.

49. Quoted in Kim Lockhart, "Drew Barrymore: Princess of the Big Screen," *Teen,* January 1999, p. 45.

50. Quoted in Brooks, "Never Been Better," p. 54.

51. Quoted in Rohrer, "True Drew," p. 295.

Chapter 6: Hollywood's Princess

52. *People Weekly,* "Ever After," August 10, 1998, p. 31.

53. Quoted in Lockhart, "Drew Barrymore," p. 44.

54. *People Weekly,* "Ever After," p. 31.

55. Quoted in Rohrer, "True Drew," *InStyle,* p. 294.

56. Quoted in van Meterm, "Drew on Top," p. 183.

57. Quoted in Brooks, "Never Been Better," p. 50.

58. Quoted in Todd Gold and J. D. Heyman, "Drew Barrymore and Tom Green Engaged," *US Weekly,* July 31, 2000, p. 27.

59. Quoted in Gold and Heyman, "Drew Barrymore and Tom Green Engaged," p. 28.

60. Quoted in Gold and Heyman, "Drew Barrymore and Tom Green Engaged," p. 27.

61. Quoted in *InStyle,* "What's Sexy Now," September 2000, p. 630.

62. Quoted in *InStyle,* "What's Sexy Now," p. 630.

63. Quoted in Rohrer, "True Drew," p. 630.

64. Quoted in Sean M. Smith, "A Whole New Drew," *Premiere,* November 2000, p. 74.

65. Quoted in Linda Friedman, "They're No Angels," *Teen People,* November 2000, p. 76.

66. Quoted in Friedman, "They're No Angels," p. 76.

67. Quoted in Sahn and Shapiro, "You Know It's Drew," p. 142.

68. Quoted in Trish Deitch Rohrer, "Watching the Detectives," *Premiere,* September 2000, p. 64.

69. Quoted in Smith, "A Whole New Drew," p. 75.

70. Quoted in Sahn and Shapiro, "You Know It's Drew," p. 147.

71. Quoted in Lockhart, "Drew Barrymore," p. 46.
72. Quoted in *Movieline*, "The Wages of Fame," May 2000, p. 58.
73. Quoted in Rohrer, "True Drew," p. 294.

Important Dates in the Life of Drew Barrymore

1975
Drew Blythe Barrymore is born on February 22 to John Barrymore Jr. and Ildyko Jaid Mako; her parents separate before she is born.

1976
Appears in first television commercial.

1978
Appears in first television movie, *Suddenly Love*.

1980
Appears in first feature film, *Altered States*.

1982
Costars in *E.T. the Extra-Terrestrial;* becomes a celebrity.

1984
Stars in *Irreconcilable Differences* and *Firestarter;* begins drinking and smoking.

1986
Tries marijuana.

1988
Begins using cocaine; enters ASAP Family Treatment Center on two separate occasions.

1989
Films television special *Fifteen and Getting Straight;* moves into her own apartment; returns to rehab for the third and final time after she slashes her wrist; moves in with Jan Dance and David Crosby after her release.

1990

Publishes best-selling autobiography, *Little Girl Lost;* obtains legal divorce from her parents.

1992

Stars in television series *2000 Malibu Road.*

1994

Marries and divorces Jeremy Thomas; founds her own production company, Flower Films.

1997

Costars in Woody Allen's musical *Everyone Says I Love You;* Flower Films signs a two-year deal with Fox Pictures 2000.

1999

Produces and stars in *Never Been Kissed;* is nominated for an American Comedy Award and Blockbuster Entertainment Award for *The Wedding Singer;* is nominated for Blockbuster Entertainment Award for *Ever After.*

2000

Receives ShoWest award for best comedian; produces and stars in *Charlie's Angels;* becomes engaged to comedian Tom Green.

For Further Reading

Books

Virginia Aronson, *Drew Barrymore*. Philadelphia: Chelsea House, 2000. This young adult biography offers a good overall view of Barrymore's life and career. It includes black-and-white photographs and a full filmography.

Drew Barrymore with Todd Gold, *Little Girl Lost*. New York: Simon & Schuster, 1990. Barrymore's own revealing autobiography was written when she was just fourteen. It has a black-and-white photo section and offers the complete story of Barrymore's struggle with addiction.

Margot Peters, *The House of Barrymore*. New York: Alfred A. Knopf, 1990. A complete look at the history of the Barrymore family.

Periodicals

Amy Brooks, "Never Been Better," *Teen People*, May 1999.

Kim Lockhart, "Drew Barrymore: Princess of the Big Screen," *Teen*, January 1999.

Trish Deitch Rohrer, "True Drew," *InStyle*, March 1999.

Works Consulted

Books

Diana Barrymore with Gerald Frank, *Too Much, Too Soon.* New York: Henry Holt, 1975. An autobiography by Drew's aunt, an actress who underwent treatment for drug and alcohol abuse before she died at age 38.

Ethel Barrymore, *Memories: An Autobiography.* New York: Harper & Brothers, 1955. An autobiography by Drew's aunt, Ethel Barrymore.

John Barrymore, *Confessions of an Actor.* Indianapolis: Bobbs-Merill, 1926. An autobiography by Drew's grandfather, John Barrymore.

Lionel Barrymore and Cameron Shipp, *We Barrymores.* New York: Appleton-Century-Crofts, 1951. An autobiography by Drew's great-uncle, Lionel Barrymore.

John Drew Jr., *My Years on the Stage.* New York: Dutton, 1922. An autobiography by Drew's grandfather's uncle.

Periodicals

Chuck Arnold, "Bad Boys," *People Weekly*, February 2, 1998.

Susanne Ault, "ShoWest Taps Carrey, Barrymore, Minghella," *Variety*, January 24, 2000.

Trish Dietch Rohrer, "True Drew," *InStyle*, November 2000.

Entertainment Weekly, "The Shoe Fits," March 5, 1999.

Linda Friedman, "They're No Angels," *Teen People,* November 2000.

Todd Gold and J. D. Heyman, "Drew Barrymore and Tom Green Engaged," *US Weekly*, July 31, 2000.

InStyle, "What's Sexy Now," September 2000.

Jonathan van Meterm, "Drew on Top," *Harper's Bazaar*, December, 1996.

Holly Millea, "Drew's Rules," *Premiere*, September 1998.

Movieline, "The Wages of Fame," May 2000.

People Weekly, "Ever After," August 10, 1998.

————, "50 Most Beautiful People in the World," May 12, 1997.

————, "Young and Hot: Top 10 Players Under 35," November 18, 1996.

Chris Petrikin, "Flower Power Re-Upped at Fox 2000," *Variety,* July 12, 1999.

Trish Deitch Rohrer, "Watching the Detectives," *Premiere,* September 2000.

Leah Rozen, "*The Wedding Singer,*" *People Weekly*, February 16, 1998.

Sarah Saffian, "Pistol-Packin' Mama," *US Weekly*, June 5, 2000.

Geri Sahn and Michele Shapiro, "You Know It's Drew," *Seventeen*, October 2000.

Lisa Schwarzbaum, "Class Dismissed," *Entertainment Weekly*, April 16, 1999.

Kyle Smith and Julie Jordan, "In *Home Fries* and at Home, Luke Wilson Sizzles with Drew Barrymore," *People Weekly*, December 7, 1998.

Sean M. Smith, "A Whole New Drew," *Premiere*, November 2000.

Bob Strauss, "It Had to Be Drew," *Entertainment Weekly,* January 24, 1997.

Teen People, "25 Hottest Stars Under 25," March 2000.

Index

Picture Credits

About the Author

Anne E. Hill has been writing for kids and teens since she was sixteen. Now, ten years later, she is a freelance writer, editor, and the author of seven books: *Denzel Washington*, which was named one of the New York Public Library's Best Books for Teenagers; *Ekaterina Gordeeva; Female Firsts in Their Fields: Broadcasting and Journalism; Cameron Diaz; Jennifer Lopez; Sergei Grinkov;* and *Sandra Bullock*. Hill is also a writer and voicer for the Concert Connection's All-Star Teen Line. She is currently writing for a popular line of teen fiction as well as biographies of actress Gwyneth Paltrow and a collective on American movie directors.

Hill graduated magna cum laude with a bachelor's degree in English from Franklin and Marshall College, where she was a member of the Phi Beta Kappa Society, an undergraduate honors organization, and wrote for the *Franklin and Marshall Magazine*. She lives near Philadelphia, Pennsylvania, with her husband, George. Her favorite Drew Barrymore film is *Ever After*.